IF WE ARE NOT IN HARMONY WITH OURSELVES, HOW CAN WE POSSIBLY BE IN HARMONY WITH THE WORLD WE INHABIT?

I am learning that it is my choice to perceive the world in a more optimistic and positive light because it is also my choice to perceive myself that way. Every single day is a lesson in the old adage that the transformation of the world we see begins with the transformation of how we see ourselves. Everything begins at home and the choices we make within the Self.

I am shifting from feelings of helplessness about having any effect in helping to change the world to a position that recognizes the power within me. A great awakening is taking place. Individuals all across the world are tapping in to their internal power to elevate their lives to a higher octave of happiness and productivity. Sharing the search, and the techniques of searching, is only a part of the help we can give one another. *Going Within* offers keys for enlightening one's inner perceptions. It is a kind of personal road map to achieving spiritual clarity.

Books by Shirley MacLaine

DANCING IN THE LIGHT
"DON'T FALL OFF THE MOUNTAIN"
IT'S ALL IN THE PLAYING
OUT ON A LIMB
YOU CAN GET THERE FROM HERE

Going Within

A GUIDE FOR INNER TRANSFORMATION

Shirley MacLaine

BANTAM BOOKS

NEW YORK · TORONTO · LONDON · SYDNEY · AUCKLAND

GOING WITHIN
A BANTAM BOOK 0 553 40048 7

Originally published in Great Britain by
Bantam Press Ltd, a division of
Transworld Publishers Ltd

PRINTING HISTORY
Bantam Press edition published 1989
Bantam Books edition published 1990

Bantam Books are published by Transworld Publishers
Ltd., 61–63 Uxbridge Road, Ealing, London W5 5SA, in
Australia by Transworld Publishers (Australia) Pty. Ltd.,
15–23 Helles Avenue, Moorebank, NSW 2170, and in New
Zealand by Transworld Publishers (N.Z.) Ltd., Cnr. Moselle
and Waipareira Avenues, Henderson, Auckland.

Printed and bound in Great Britain by
Cox & Wyman Ltd., Reading, Berks.

For

Sachi
Mother
Kathleen
and
Bella
and all the other women *and* men who seek
the spiritual feminine in themselves

And for
Ian and Betty Ballantine,
who were there from the beginning

One should start with oneself
But never end with oneself.

Contents

Author's Preface

I have been having an extraordinary adventure for the past seven years. Some would call it an adventure in cosmic consciousness, and while I would agree with that, I would also add that it is an adventure which enjoys the advantage of extremely pragmatic, down-to-earth application in real life.

I am learning that it is my choice to perceive the world in a more optimistic and positive light because I am learning that it is also my choice to perceive myself that way. Every single day is a lesson in the old adage that the transformation of the world we see begins with the transformation of how we see ourselves. Everything begins at home and the choices we make within the Self.

I used to hear these words and privately feel that

this was simple "selfishness" or even dangerously self-centered fantasy. No longer. To me, this concept has become a giant truth. "Know thyself"—and everything else follows. In fact I now realize that it is impossible for me to understand anything of the world, its inhabitants, their suffering, their conflicts or the full potential of life itself until I am in touch with these same currents and truths inside myself. To understand and love others begins with understanding and loving oneself.

These are issues of the spirit, not of the mind and body. When I began the investigation of understanding the spiritual aspect of my nature *and* that of everyone else, the missing pieces of the puzzle of the human condition began to fall into place.

The study took work, discipline, and a concentrated effort in unraveling the ancient techniques of what I call spiritual technology. The more I applied the tools of what I investigated, the more I found my own experience, my own attitudes, and my own perceptions transforming my life into a more positive and peaceful adventure.

As the millenium approaches and a new century beckons, the complications of living are becoming more challenging. Millions of people all over the world are seeking to transform and improve their lives. They are painfully aware that the answers for a changed world are not coming from sources outside of themselves. The answers lie within.

That is what this book is about. GOING WITHIN

offers keys for enlightening one's inner perceptions. It is a kind of personal roadmap for achieving spiritual clarity that can make the transformation in inner attitude improve outer reality. Hopefully my own search, with its methods, techniques, and new approaches, can be helpful to those who are also seeking to reduce conflict, anger, confusion and stress in their lives.

This book grew out of the year I spent criss-crossing the country conducting seminars on inner transformation. Never before had I spent such quality time with so many people engaged in their own desire for improvement. The intense, face-to-face contact and sharing of deep, powerful and honest emotional struggles in our dangerously complicated world helped me articulate and shape the journey I was making myself. Together we became more skilled in the techniques of meditation and visualization. Together we deepened our understanding of our intuitive gifts and of the body's esoteric centers of energy and their role in both physical and emotional healing. Together we strengthened our belief that each one of us has the responsibility to create the world in which we choose to live.

I don't expect that any of us will succeed in transforming ourselves into a state of peaceful bliss in this lifetime. But each one of us *can* help to leave a better world fit for our children to live in, a world that is more trusting in the belief that inside each of us is a wealth of power to learn how to love and to change.

This is indeed a difficult and sometimes threatening time for all of us. But it is also an astonishing opportunity for growth if we choose to look at it that way. The very urgency of the need for change will accelerate the metamorphosis required to proceed into the next century and the next millenium.

The longest journey begins with the first step. Perhaps the longest journey is the journey within. It is never too late to begin.

1
The Seminar

*The person who knows how to laugh at himself
will never cease to be amused.*

I walked into the Grand Ballroom, down the center aisle, lightly touched the wireless microphone nestled neatly into my sweater at the throat, cleared my voice, braced my shoulders, and climbed onto the makeshift stage.

I turned around and looked out into the faces of fifteen hundred people who had come to experience a weekend of spiritual investigation with me.

I would be standing on this stage for about eighteen hours, with no real idea of the emotional and spiritual needs and questions of the crowd until they spontaneously expressed themselves. Knowing from professional experience that every audience is different, I was still aware that this was no ordinary audience. This was a collective of individuals, every single one of whom had a story and a prior life and a particular need that had brought him or her to this place at this time. It was anybody's guess what would happen. I stood before them, wondering what they would do.

As I looked out over the crowd I was suddenly stunned at the fact that my life had brought me to this point. In a timeless moment I flashed back to myself as a small girl of three, wearing a four-leaf-clover hat, with an apple clutched firmly in hand as I faced an audience to sing "An Apple for the Teacher." Had I begun as a performer even then in order to perfect the craft of communication so that fifty years later I could attempt to make simple sense of complicated concepts of spirituality? Had it all been leading to this? I took a deep breath.

I've always known that I am basically a communicating performer—that is, someone more challenged on a stage than in the safe environment of a movie studio. I need personal contact with others. I need to know how I am doing. And now I needed to "feel" others who were on the same path as I was. The letters, phone calls, and interviews that had resulted from my books and my *Out on a Limb* miniseries were not sufficient now. I needed to go deeper, in myself as well as with others who also wanted to explore within themselves. I was hungry for an exchange that would be mutually helpful.

I studied their faces and reflected upon what had brought us all here. I was about to conduct a series of weekend seminars all across America, having chosen this method of communication because it was personal and because I wanted to give back some of the knowledge I had been privileged to gain from others much more evolved and educated than myself. I wanted to be with people who were working seriously on their own searches. I also secretly wanted to find out if it was really possible to communicate such esoteric concepts in a structured manner that would make pragmatic and logical sense. Could we, among us, bring spiritual questions down to Earth?

This very question has been responsible for my doubts, even fear, of having to give up my professional approach to presentation. By that I mean I always needed to feel prepared and well rehearsed before I appeared in front of people. I needed to learn a prepared text when I made a speech; I needed to know my lines before I sang a song or acted a scene. I had always carefully prepared my shows, with an orchestra, backup dancers, and all the highly skilled hoopla of costumes and lighting that are the building blocks of such a show. And even though, invariably, extemporaneous material arose out of the varying reactions of each audience, I was comfortable with ad-libbing in that situation because the spontaneity arose out of knowing what I was doing.

But here I would be on a bare stage with nothing to present but myself, the knowledge I had gleaned over the years, and my thoughts on esoteric, far-out concepts, based on strong personal experience.

❈

And now, here I stood. I felt naked and vulnerable before the crowd of people, except for the twenty-five-page security blanket of a speech clutched in my hands. I looked out at them as they settled and hushed. Suddenly I knew I would lose this audience if I referred to that speech even once.

So I made a decision. After acknowledging their applause, I put the speech down on the table behind me. I took another deep breath, and stood, waiting. The room became very still, currents of silent energy hovering, waiting. With my eyes wide open, I meditated, asking for help. I knew I had guides and teachers. They might reside in an unseen dimension but they were nevertheless very real to me. I allowed myself to believe that I was aligning with them and with a spiritual dimension that could see me through whatever was required to make pragmatic sense to everyone in the audience.

Many, many thoughts went through my mind in what was, in fact, a very brief time, but in that time, power seemed to flow into me and through me. I began to feel imbued with confidence. It was a glorious feeling. Not arrogant but richly confident.

Feeling relaxed, centered, and certain, somewhere in my being, that nothing could go wrong, I knew I would be able to keep a hard-edged grip on the esoteric material. I actually began to experience a new vibration of harmony in my body as well. My sense of urgency left me. With the relaxation came a feeling of humor, a lightness of heart. I felt no worry, no tension, as though I was floating in the warmth of friends. I thought of other situations in my life when I had been tense, anxious, and even downright terrified. If only I had known about meditating for help from a dimension of spirituality. It would have been so much easier and more productive.

More than anything else, I felt no sense of time, as though I would be living the entire weekend as a whole, that the clock would not matter at all, that I would be experiencing an inner time. Yet, I was aware that I would cover each area of material within reasonable time parameters, that I would call lunch breaks (and kidney breaks) at appropriate intervals, that I would pace myself and the people with me so that we would all gain from the experience. In short, I felt a new professional trust.

I would be able to extend the joy of live communication to include the mysteries of spiritual realms. Together we would pursue those dimensions and trust that our motivations were based on that ever-deepening quest to know self.

There have been a few times in my acting and performing career when I have felt such a keen sense of harmonious elation. These were times when the energy flow was so rich, so full, so *total*, that I could simply "go" with the security of what was happening, and completely surrender to the sheer joy of what I was doing.

That is exactly what happened at that first seminar, and, with variations, continued to happen through the year of seminars that followed.

Something else happened. I realized that people were coming because each person wanted to connect with his or her own higher power and they felt there was more to their potential for this connection than they had been able to reach alone. They knew that working together with large groups could accelerate the process because the energy in the room was intensified. Thus I became aware that there was a new movement growing; that people wanted to work together, share together, investigate together, and heal themselves together. For far too long they had felt isolated in their conflicts. If we were going to improve ourselves and the world, we would have to learn to love, respect, and work together in order to achieve that goal.

As I traveled the country I found that thousands of people were opening up and surrendering to their own internal spiritual power, the power that lay waiting for them to access and enjoy in each other.

People had grown wary of giving their power to outside gurus and teachers and were ready to reassume their own internal authority, to work within themselves.

They knew *they* were going to have to do the work, that I was not a guru or a teacher, that I could only share experience, gently lead and suggest, relate what I had done and what I had gained from it, in the hope that that would help them to find their own strengths. They knew that I was attempting to find my way just as they were finding theirs.

Never in all my years of public life had I met such intelligent and courageous people. People from all walks of life—doctors, scientists, psychiatrists, homemakers, business executives, even politicians. All were stretching their vistas of truth. They had come, undaunted by raised eyebrows, snickers, and sometimes downright ridicule—each one seemed to have experienced the colorful family dramas that apparently accompany every self-search. They seemed glad, indeed delighted, to be able to talk freely about their beliefs, their doubts, their traumas, their questions, and their triumphs. One man said he was learning to fly an airplane because he was taking himself more lightly!

Each of the seminars produced hundreds of stories, each a real-life drama, nor were any feelings held back. I was amazed, and I felt gifted, and grateful for the trust we were able to exchange.

We laughed together about the reactions of friends and family, some of whom did not always understand, and soon it was clear that nothing demeaning or tragic could really happen, other than serving as a catalyst for a very rich vein of metaphysical humor to be mined by Johnny Carson and comics everywhere.

We did not care. The world needed some fresh laughs anyway.

People came bearing crystals, books, handmade presents, candy, carrot cake, even frankincense and myrrh, a wonderful combined incense. Gifts, for me and for each other. At first I had a problem accepting such gifts, feeling that the people were giving their power to me, but one of the great lessons was not only to learn to accept love and expressions of it even from strangers, but to look at how arrogant it was of me to believe that my power was in danger of usurping theirs!

In company with a thousand strangers, people openly trusted in spiritual sharing and talked freely about their heretofore closely guarded secrets. They knew no trust would be betrayed. We meditated together. On inner personal levels we contacted departed loved ones together. We talked about fear, evil, how to learn to love more unconditionally—and always there was the trust in ourselves and one another.

They came with pillows to use when sitting on the floor, with notepaper, and with open hearts. We learned early on to understand the theory of power present when three or more people gathered in the name of universal Divine Energy. Perhaps it was the cosmic triad—one for mind, one for body, one for spirit. In any case, the more people there were, the more each person's inner power was increased. Sometimes the energy in the room was so intense it could actually be seen by the "sensitives" attending. If there were one thousand individual souls working with nonfragmented, focused intention in the same room, the power of that collective-soul energy became one colossal vibration.

There were many beginners who had never meditated or visualized in their lives. The more advanced people often learned a great deal from the beginners because they were so pure and uneducated about metaphysics. One can become as intellectually arrogant about spirituality as about empirical science.

So everyone worked together to allow themselves to let go. I discouraged note-taking, and tape recorders were not allowed, not only because it disturbed others but because such techniques blocked the process of absorbing the information through the heart and the feelings. These devices focused on the mind instead, which was in direct opposition to what we were attempting to achieve—a wholeness of concentration that included body, mind, and spirit. At first I'd notice a momentary expression of panic when people had to put down their pads and pencils, but soon their faces became less strained, more relaxed, and ultimately full of wonder about what they were feeling in themselves.

After a question-and-answer period during which people realized they had many problems in common and which allowed them to get to know one another, I guided a collective meditation, using natural sound effects of birds, bubbly flowing streams, soft breezes, crystals gently tinkling, and music that promoted a feeling of well-being and peace.

These collective meditations, some lasting as long as two hours, were often deeply cathartic for many people (including myself), because we were making contact with a very personal essence that I can only describe as being connected to the Divine. When that connection is felt, the result opens floodgates of insight and well-being. Emotional catharsis is in itself a practical aid to solving personal problems and reducing stress.

The study of spirituality and metaphysics, therefore, is motivated by extremely pragmatic considerations, particularly with respect to improving one's performance in life, and hence one's feeling of well-being. Emotional catharsis can also create a climate for clarity of thought, enabling one to confront complex problems, both internal and external, allowing priorities to emerge that can then be resolved, or at least put into perspective. Such a study is not at all an exercise in fantasy—at least not in my experience. Going within, touching one's inner self, holds solutions for many people for whom nothing else seems to work. And going within in a collective environment carries with it an extraordinary power, because everyone is working and meditating with the same intention; there is no fragmentation of focus. Each individual in the room trusts that there is a higher power in himself or herself as well as in everyone else. As a result, the process of connecting with that power is accelerated.

There we'd be, in the Grand Ballroom of some hotel in a large city, at the center of urban plastic and concrete. Next door the Shriners might be having a convention.

We were so silent that often someone from outside would open a door and peer in, wondering if the Grand Ballroom was indeed occupied. In meditation, our people were absorbed, enthralled in the exploration of themselves, coming to terms with and clearing out whatever they needed to in their lives.

I'd ask them to picture themselves with someone they felt had hurt them more than any other, then to go deep into the soul level of communication and ask that person why the hurt had been necessary. Nearly everyone got an "answer." And apparently the answers were of such significance that most people allowed themselves to weep openly about that hurtful experience for the first time in their lives. On some soul level they were talking to the person in question. People thus confronted their own anger, their feelings of abandonment, rejection, and loneliness. And through the courage of confrontation they became more illumined, clearer about their personal motivations.

They all wanted to talk, to share their internal experiences. Problems held in common with others opened up areas for animated discussions with one another. (Indeed, many friendships were sparked by these seminars, and later cemented into lasting relationships.)

The stories that people related were astonishing in their frankness. One woman told the group she had understood and forgiven a man who had raped her. A man understood why his father had beaten him. A young woman understood and forgave her mother for abandoning her at the age of seven. The stories and personal dramas were touching, alarming, funny— and the resolutions infinitely satisfying. People trusted the concept that they could indeed clear out their emotional pain by going within themselves. They trusted the idea that on that same deep soul level they could connect with the soul of another human being. Soon they saw that the clearing had everything to do with how *they* perceived the problem and nothing to do with the person whom they had previously perceived to have inflicted pain upon them.

Sometimes, while guiding the meditations, I would proceed involuntarily to clear out some of my own pain. Whenever that happened, I found myself crying, having lost my control in the collective experience. I had as much to clear as everybody else and it was temptingly easy to flow into the collective energy because it was so powerfully accessible. But I could not afford to lose myself without losing the group. So I found that I needed to do my own clearing privately, alone, either in my room during lunch break or at night when I was finished with the seminar.

The seminars were continuously productive of insights, humor, warmly touching experiences with thousands of people—a constant ebb and flow of energy that was always rewarding. What was most interesting was that I was *never* tired. As a matter of fact, the residue of the weekend-seminar energy stayed with me until Wednesday of each week, whereupon the dissipation left me bereft and I longed for the next weekend to come sooner. A description of the "energy" is difficult. I can only say it had something to do with feeling I was inside a "spiritual, God-source vibration." I knew we were collectively accessing the spiritual realms when we meditated together, but it was as though we each acknowledged that our guides and teachers were present and helping us in a way more gently powerful than we had previously had the nerve to admit.

Before embarking on the seminars I was concerned about conducting them without benefit of a degree or a license of some kind. There wasn't much I could do about it, however, because there are no degrees or credentials in spirituality or metaphysics, which is interesting in itself. Actually, some courses in philosophy, physics, mathematics, and transpersonal psychology come close—which is also interesting. I remember how my father talked about discussing "unseen truths" when he was a student and a professor of psychology and philosophy at Johns Hopkins

University. "We all respected traditional education along these lines," he would say, "but we also *knew* there was something more."

Just before the seminars began, my father passed on. He had been a teacher all his life. I considered canceling the first few dates but I knew he would have wanted me to carry on.

So I found myself, by no small coincidence, in Virginia Beach, staying in the same hotel to which my father had brought us on vacation during a summer that provided a self-conscious twelve-year-old with a traumatic experience. It had to do with public humiliation.

I was swimming in the Atlantic, having developed a crush on the lifeguard, when a surging wave knocked me over and the top of my two-piece bathing suit came apart and was washed away. I climbed to my knees sputtering but glad to be alive, until I looked down and saw that I was exposed to the lifeguard in all my teenage splendor. I was so embarrassed I wanted to die. He smiled, which made it even worse. I ran back to the hotel. For years, Virginia Beach and a pounding surf were a combination that made me inwardly cringe.

As I stood looking out at the same beach, the same surf, from the same hotel, I realized I would, as an adult, be dealing with the same issue—potential public humiliation.

It was all tied in with my father somehow. He had been an innovative teacher but had also been concerned with what people thought. In fact, "social appropriateness" had deterred his growth and blunted his courage. I wasn't going to let that happen to me. I wanted to be myself regardless of what anybody thought. I turned away from the window and went down to the hotel ballroom. The seminar was a great success. All the time, I felt that my father was with me, helping me from the other side as I embarked on a new form of audience participation. There were moments when I felt him guide me as to what to say next, how to make a transition, how to express my thoughts. It was as though, from his vantage point, he now realized there was no point in worrying about what others thought. He was telling me to be true to myself. At the end of the weekend, Virginia Beach was snowed in and as a result no one could get out of town. Mini-seminars sprang up in hallways and restaurants. I stood at my hotel window looking out at the windswept beach where I had been mortified at losing my bathing-suit top. I felt my father beside me. "So much for hu-miliation," I said to myself. I felt him nod in agreement.

Each city had its own "feeling," its own rhythms, its own pace—and its own peculiarities.

In San Diego my own people wouldn't let me into the ballroom because I wasn't wearing an ID badge.

In Seattle a woman swooned with ecstasy during a meditation, whereupon one of our Facilitators called the paramedics, who brought the police. TV cameras were outside waiting for any bit of cosmic scandal, but Midge Costanza, my able administrative assistant, put herself in front of the door and said, "You'll go in there and ruin the meditation in progress over my dead body." She didn't need to die. They left.

In San Francisco we were at the Moscone Center and someone put up flags flying outside that correctly matched the order of the chakra colors we visualized as an exercise. "Cosmic patriotism," someone said. After the first chanting meditation, my driver, who sat in on the seminar, remarked, "You know, I believe Om is where the heart is."

I, in the meantime, was experiencing the rigors and discomfort of a temporary bridge that had fallen out of my mouth (times for visits to my dentist were few and far between). A local dentist from San Francisco showed up in my hotel room. He was gay, but was wearing rubber gloves. That night I spoke at an AIDS dinner (trying to hold in my bridge as I spoke), associating and interrelating with many people who were suffering from AIDS. San Francisco provided me with an opportunity to test my own spirituality and trust that there was nothing to fear and that my teeth would stay in besides.

In Boston we had union problems with workers who wouldn't set up the room in time. They said it shouldn't matter to us because we could just levitate through the day. A reporter who was attending from New York City wrote that his experience in connecting with his Higher Self had been intriguing, since it occurred at two-thirty in the afternoon and he hadn't yet had lunch. His Higher Self turned out to be a thick steak and some french fries.

Along with the other problems we had a group of "Future Citizens of America" in a convention room next to our meditating spiritual seekers. They were young adults (whatever that means) and thought it was amusing to rap on the doors of our ballroom and try to crack our concentration. "We thought you'd be out of your bodies and wouldn't hear us," said one future CIA operative. I told him maybe I was out of my body, but he was out of his mind. He ceased and desisted.

In Albuquerque I forgot all my notes. I left them on the airplane. Even though I hadn't used them, they were there for me to refer to as support and preparation. I panicked and became very depressed until I finally got myself together and realized I must have forgotten them purposely, for a good reason. From then on I worked *entirely* spontaneously and found it a very pleasurable experience and the people responded even more.

In Chicago there were so many people (nearly fifteen hundred) that we couldn't seat them all in festival fashion on the floor. There was a jovial Bar

Mitzvah going on next door and the celebrating and music filtered through the walls. I didn't think anything would work. I suggested that everyone go into a meditation and ask for help. The music immediately stopped and somehow there was room for everybody to either sit on the floor or find chairs along walls. Judeo-Christian guidance, you might say.

In Los Angeles there were many journalists attending who were there not for reporting but for personal learning. One of them, from the *Los Angeles Times,* stood up and said, "Since I've been working with my higher power I've changed my life and my journalistic work has improved." She added, "So I think newspaper editors would do well to rely more on the Source rather than their sources!" She got a big hand.

New York City (both times) was the most serious and committed group. It was always the largest and the most quiet. Bella Abzug and some of her political staff were there, the press following them around saying, "You believe all this stuff now?" She responded by saying, "Shirley's my friend and I always consider seriously whatever she does." Several journalists wrote good, well-informed pieces.

In Dallas something incredible (even from my viewpoint) occurred. The water in the Fairmont Hotel was cut off due to a break in a water main. Water was gushing out into the street. I suggested to my crowd that we do a meditation visualizing the water backing up so that the workers could find the break. Right after that collective visualization the electric power went out. I had no microphone, the air conditioner shut down, and there were no lights. Since I was running late anyway, I brought that day's seminar to a close and went outside to see what was wrong. On the street in front of the hotel the workers said, "The strangest thing just happened. The water out here suddenly stopped flowing, then it backed up and flooded the basement of the hotel until it covered the electrical transformer, which caused the power blackout." I nodded and said it was all too bad. To me this was an example of the power of collective visualization. I was careful, after that, about how I used it.

The following week, in another Los Angeles seminar, every time I came near an elevator the power went out. I kept the crowd waiting fifteen minutes because I couldn't get into an elevator that worked! I do not know why this happened and continues to happen to me on some level with electrical equipment. In fact, the night I saw *Phantom of the Opera* in London, the chandelier that was supposed to "fall" over the audience and crash onto the stage didn't work! The manager of the theater said that had never happened before.

On reflection, I think that every time electronic

equipment fails around me it is because I am feeling distorted and out of alignment. I *am* developing my power but I also have a long way to go. Hence, developing one's inner power requires the responsibility to go all the way. Each of the times electronic equipment became distorted was a time when *I* felt out of "sync." I was either anxious or nervous or worried.

In Washington, D.C., I sat in my hotel room with Senator Claiborne Pell (chairman of the Senate Foreign Relations Committee), the Duke of Liechtenstein, Bella Abzug, and several people from Congress as we listened to Whitley Streiber (*Communion*) and Bud Hopkins (*The Intruders*) talk about their experiences with UFOs. Hopkins had brought a girl with him who claimed that she had been impregnated invisibly by an extraterrestrial. She said she had brought the baby to term, only to have it dematerialized by the ETs before she could see it. The doctors were as shocked as she because the fetus *had* been there and disappeared. However, they weren't as shocked as the politicians listening to the story, who were perhaps beginning to realize that there was an entirely separate reality occurring in America that could somehow impact on the political system. I was amused as we sat there listening to the story of a disappearing fetus. "I wonder how Phyllis Schafly would handle that," said Bella. She added, "Congress was never like this."

During the seminars, I was learning to work with my feminine spiritual energy, learning to trust it more than I ever had. And I knew the experience would profoundly affect my approach to my profession as an actress and performer. The feminine energy was that of allowance, trust, and tolerance. I was *letting* myself trust that everything would go well if I just got out of my own way. I consciously caught myself feeling anxiety and stress, and *stopped*. That meant giving up old professional approaches to public appearances. As a result, I had a love affair with the "moment." I had read so much about living in the moment—appreciating the NOW. I finally challenged myself to understand what that was all about. And I loved it. Life itself was all about NOW, I came to realize, not about the past or future. If I worried about what I might have done in the past, or what I might do in the future, the NOW suffered. So I set about expanding my concept and boundaries of NOW. Because of that perspective, I never got tired. Exhaustion was foreign to me. I could have gone on for hours. Of course I loved the material and never lost interest in it, because of the deep concentration on what was happening in the moment and because it was such a loving involvement. Many business executives told me that their therapists had encouraged them to attend because meditation itself was so helpful in reducing stress in their lives. Allowing themselves the fulfillment of the moment helped them to relax and become more productive.

As the seminars drew to a close, I was amazed at how many people had been willing to look at the multi-dimensionality of themselves. It was as though the old concepts of self didn't work anymore. Those concepts were too limited. On a fundamental level people *knew* that they were more than they seemed or had been taught. I was proud to have contributed to that knowledge. But the truth of it is, every one of those people was a teacher for *me*. They had taught me to channel my own spiritual power, and I had only begun.

One month after the seminars ended, I went back to work as an actress. And I used some of my spiritual techniques from the seminars in my acting. I found an epic character in a picture called *Madame Sousatzka,* directed by John Schlesinger. Madame Sousatzka was a part and a half: a domineering teacher of classical piano; commanding, manipulative, outrageous, funny, vulnerable, and, in the end, uplifting. Whatever my character Aurora Greenway might have been in *Terms of Endearment,* Madame Sousatzka made her look like a quiet day at the beach. As I hadn't worked since *Terms* (aside from playing myself in *Out on a Limb*), I was excited at the prospect of trying a new way of working.

I proceeded to sculpt, with Schlesinger's help, what Sousatzka looked like, what she wore, how her hair was styled, what jewelry clanked on her wrists, how she walked, talked, ate, breathed, laughed, and cried. Then I molded and refined her in my mind. She became a composite of reality; a real, living, breathing character fashioned from our creativity. After I finished my composition of thought, I let her go. I threw her up to the universe and said, "Now you play yourself through me."

I had seen so many channels and mediums over the past few years, I decided I would apply the same thing to show business. I simply put my conscious ego aside, got out of my own way, and channeled a character that we had created and I absolutely adored. We actors are continually looking for techniques to inhabit the character we are asked to play. This time I allowed the character to inhabit me. Instead of trying to become Sousatzka and wait for the inspiration of the artistic impulse to happen, I just let her play herself through me. She was a compulsive eater, so I gained fifteen pounds. She was not a woman to whom time had been kind. As I watched the dailies, my face reflected *her* ravages. I wondered if I'd ever play leading ladies again. Perhaps I would enjoy playing character parts for the rest of my life. Sousatzka had a bad back; *my* back gave me pain when I went into a scene. Sousatzka had been a great concert pianist; I found that I could learn the music after only a few hearings because *she* knew how to direct my fingers to the right keys on the piano! I trusted that the magic would work if I allowed it to and simply *let* Sousatzka live through me. The character created had become real—channeling and inspiration had become one and the same.

So my experience of channeling spiritual energy in the seminars had translated to practical film acting. Reel life and real life had merged. And both were contributing to an ever-expanding reality for me.

2

The Ancient New Age

Recognize all the parts that make the whole,
for you are the maker.

Before going into some of the techniques of what we might call spiritual technology, I would like to address myself to the thinking that is fundamental to the process of "going within." This thinking stems from what is being described as the "New Age." Much has been written about the New Age, much argued, for and against. The New Age in all its manifestations has been the rich source of many, many jokes, much conjecture, concern, and even fear.

What I find most interesting about New Age perceptions—that is, how the New Age is perceived—are the enormously fragmented points of view that it seems to generate. This argues for a lack of understanding, or, at best, fragmented forms of understanding.

I hope I can help clarify the confusion.

First of all, there's nothing new about the New

Age. It is, as has been correctly reported, a compilation of many ancient spiritual points of view relating to belief, the nature of reality, the practice of living, ritual, and truth, all predominantly originating in cultures other than those of the West. To dismiss these points of view as occult or bizarre, or to have the panic reaction that they are "satanic," is to define the degree of one's own ignorance of highly developed spiritual cultures in the Near, Middle, and Far East.

The word *occult* simply means "hidden." Much of Eastern thinking has been hidden from our view. Now that some of this knowledge is being brought to light, it appears to be speaking to a New Age—but only in the view of us Westerners. It is not so much that we are backward, but that we have a different approach, and/or that we have *forgotten* some of our own early teachings.

So let's go back a bit to New Age origins.

Christian Gnostics operated with New Age knowledge and thinking for hundreds of years after the death of Christ. In fact, *gnosis* means "knowledge." But the Gnostics eventually separated from the authority of what had become a ritualized Christian Church because they believed that man's destiny was an individual matter between himself and God, not a matter for the authority of the Church to decide.

Personal responsibility is an awesome load for an individual to assume. It is obviously far easier to leave matters of conscience, God, faith, moral behavior, lifestyle, and even life-and-death decisions to some vaguely authorized power of church or government. However, though easier, clearly such a state of dependence is not a healthy one, particularly when the values and moral behavior of those in authority are as questionable as we all know they are today.

Many people these days are finding that life has become confused, tense, anxiety-riddled, and somehow lacking in purpose, because they are not using their own internal strengths to solve their problems. People speak of stress as being unbearable. They are beginning to claim that material wealth, success, fame, and the accepted avenues of over-achievement are no longer fulfilling, indeed are not worth the stress they engender. *There has to be something more* is a refrain all too often echoed.

Intelligent and well-intentioned people look around and see an agglomeration of undeclared wars being bloodily fought, the virulence of nuclear power competition, a drug-ridden world, the horrifying spectacle of millions of malnourished and even more millions of illiterates in the richest nation in the world, vaulting rates of violent crime and fatal disease, the insane poisoning of our environment—a veritable litany of disaster and self-destruction—and ask, not unnaturally, what the hell is happening to the human race? Why are people doing this?

If those same intelligent questioners would go just a little bit further, and ask, "Why are *we* doing this *to ourselves*?" they would be thinking in New Age terms.

Because the New Age is all about *self*-responsibility. New Age thinking asks that each person take responsibility for everything that happens in life because everything in life is connected. But the very first responsibility has to be personal—in a totally real sense, care for one's Self.

This is not easy. It requires self-reflection and self-confrontation of the first order. It means looking in the mirror and forgiving oneself for *not* acknowledging that out of love for oneself can come love for others and ultimately love for the world we live in. From that loving self-realization can come solutions to the horrific problems *we* have created.

Critics point out that the New Age is a movement focused on the optimum development of one's own potential while the rest of the world and its problems lie unattended; that in the success of the New Age we risk losing some of society's best and brightest to the seduction of self. One wonders what we should lose such individuals to—high-tech warfare research, for instance? The *point* is that a great many of the horrors we live among exist precisely because we have neglected to recognize and celebrate and utilize the positive strengths within ourselves—we have neglected self-love. And the truth is that positive self-fulfillment is expressed most strongly in relation to others. What we literally cannot do is become productively involved with the rest of the world unless and until we learn to like ourselves. This then increases our ability to like and love others, which in turn augments the possibility to create change. So it is fortunate indeed that New Agers include some of the best and the brightest.

They are individuals who are profoundly concerned with what is happening to our planet and *all* the life residing on it. New Agers include antiwar activists, pro-environmentalists, antinukers, peaceniks, feminists, ecologists, bankers, psychologists, doctors, physicists, blue-, white-, and even no-collar workers, and many, many more—so there are apparently millions of people who advocate the "selfish" view of wanting to save our planet from destruction by beginning with themselves.

The person who is wound up in self-hatred, self-denigration, self-doubt, and self-contempt is suffocated, bound by a negative self-image that does not permit time or energy to really care about anyone else. Such feelings feed on themselves, generating more and more hatred, anger, and resentment, which will almost inevitably spill over onto others.

There is no question that modern-day psychologists are deeply concerned by the degree of violence vibrating under the surface behavior of most human beings—and increasingly emerging as expressed violence and self-destructiveness. They claim that the only way to solve the conflicts that pressurize our culture is to help people confront the underlying causes of their violence. When one understands the real cause for feelings of hatred and anger, one can change the feelings, or even let them go. That involves taking responsibility for what we feel. It means we have to stop blaming others for our *own* problems. It means accepting our own contribution to conflicts and unhappinesses, and becoming more consciously aware of why we feel what we do.

In doing so, we are expanding our conscious awareness, which means, to use a New Age term, that we are "raising" our consciousness about our unconscious perceptions of who we are and how we are behaving. We are learning surprising things about ourselves.

The only source is ourselves.

The so-called "cult of self" then becomes the pursuit of knowledge of self so that, upon resolution of conflicts, we can become more contributive to the society we live in.

I believe it is time to begin to heal ourselves and in so doing to help heal others in our society. The responsibility does not lie only in systems of authority like the church, the state, or the schools. The responsibility lies also in each and every one of *us*.

The family is the unit in which we begin the investigation of Self. We pick up more of our parents' attitudes on self-investigation than we think we do. Our basic orientation on self-reflection comes from the family. If our parents or caretakers didn't want to look at themselves, this can affect us deeply. Conversely, if our parents were self-reflective, we are likely to be, too. But the family unit is the synthesis for society and it is up to us to improve our own vision of ourselves within the family before we can function with a full vision outside of it. And if we are young enough, perhaps we can achieve that vision before we start our own families, and hence improve matters for the next generation.

Speaking personally, I now know that I related to my parents as I *perceived* them to be. When I began to see them as being not all-powerful but as fallible, as human beings in their own right, as *persons* with needs of their own, separate from myself—when, in short, I learned to allow them to be themselves—they no longer troubled me so much. My daughter is learning to do the same with me, and I with her. *To release others from the expectations we have of them is to really love them.* We are free of our loved ones when we care enough to let them go. And the anomaly, or so it seems, then becomes that the love bonds grow stronger. So we can honor our parents, and our selves, by growing up, by not getting stuck in some infantilized phase of blind expectation and demand, becoming frustrated, bitter, angry, and hating because the demands seem unfulfilled. In growing up, we accept responsibility for ourselves by having the courage to look at who we are and what we really want out of this life.

Whenever I ask people what they want for themselves and for the world, the answer is almost always the same—peace.

I believe peace for the world cannot be achieved without peace within our individual selves.

It seems to me that the dilemma of war, of destructiveness in all its forms, always returns to self. Personal conflict deters peace, engenders external conflict. It is impossible to feel like a complete human being as long as the fragmentation of conflict exists. Again, who creates the conflict? Again, *we* do. We are angry at those who mirror to us the unresolved aspects we possess in ourselves.

To me, this basic principle appears to be at work throughout the world. If we are not in harmony with ourselves, how can we possibly be in harmony with anyone else, much less the world we inhabit? We want to lead lives that are whole, without sorrow, anger, fear, stress, and anxiety, yet we continue to define ourselves by these negative outlooks. We seem to be ignorant of, and even threatened by, more positive perceptions. Indeed, some people would call positive perceptions sentimental or unrealistic. Intellectuals who achieve personal security only in being cynical scoff at love and the softer emotions as being mere sentimentality. Good is not in the cards for the human race, they say. Just look at our history, they say. (What they are *really* saying is, "I don't want to risk belief, or love, or anything kindly, because I can't bear to be hurt, or betrayed, or rebuffed, or made to look foolish.") The human race has indeed had a bloody history. So what do we do? Keep allowing, or *causing,* it to happen? Or try, each one of us individually, to accept the internal recognition of responsibility, to believe in and make real the power that each of us possesses, *knowing that what one single person does can indeed make a difference.*

This so-called New Age then is the age that challenges us to use our power to create whatever happiness we want and need in our lives. As many of the great teachers have said, *it takes a great deal of effort to be unhappy.* Why *not* use the effort in the other direction?

As we become more enlightened about ourselves, the more we manifest (live, act out, dispense) happiness. The more we manifest happiness, the more society will improve.

So what are some of the factors holding us back?

Up to now most of the progress defined in our society has revolved around the great advances in technology. Indeed, we have made giant strides in translating our intelligence into technology, to the benefit of a great many people, to such a degree that we are now using technology as the medium, and the measure, of our evolution. Now we are suffering the consequences of making technology a little tin God.

Technology has outstripped our knowledge of self. I remember reading a report on the world's most impoverished nation. It was researched by a Western economist. In the view of this authority, the world's most impoverished nation was the Himalayan mountain kingdom of Bhutan (a Shangri-la of a place I visited years ago). When presented with the facts of the report, the king of Bhutan said, in effect, "Bhutan may have technological impoverishment but we have spiritual richness and happiness." We clearly have different standards of measurement. The Bhutanese would wonder why man should produce any product if it reduces spirituality. We would wonder why we should be concerned with spirituality if it doesn't generate product.

Technology has become the way Western man perceives progress. But technology itself is a reflection of how we see ourselves. If the negativity is in us, it will appear somewhere in our technology. It is inescapable. Through technological progress we are moving faster and faster . . . toward what? We have taken the concept of the magic carpet and, bolt by bolt, turned it into an airplane—but the magic has gone out of it. The magic has been replaced by hurry, crowding, frustration, anger, even ulcers and heart attacks, many, many accidents, and a harried, embattled feeling of alienation from the original purpose of the magic of flying . . . to experience being above the fray.

I think we must learn to place technology in its proper framework and perspective. It is a tool for comfort for the physical betterment of *all* people—it is not a mark of evolutionary development. There is no innate wisdom in technology. No matter how sophisticated, or how clever, or how fast it is, even artificial intelligence in computer form still requires human control, the application of humane thinking. Do we really want computer-*directed* living? Some scientists are pleading for more "humanization" of

technology, warning that conscious awareness relative to what we are producing technologically is a
dire necessity if we are to avoid obliterating ourselves. They ask for a redirection of technology to
include consciousness and spirituality because without it we may well destroy the planet.

We cannot divorce what we are producing from
what we are. We create technology out of the vision
we have of ourselves. If we are blind in our conception of ourselves we will create a blind technology.
Our technology reflects disharmony with natural laws
because we ourselves are not in harmony with natural laws. The technology merely reflects our own
neuroses, our own demented drive for power, our
own sense of chaos, our distorted behavior patterns:
violence-directed mechanisms on the one hand, fran-
tic overproduction on the other. We need to free
ourselves of destructive patterning. We need to see
the logic of order, in man, in nature, in technology,
in our world. Or, as Krishnamurti said: "Order is
morality," and, "The content of our consciousness is
a product of our conditioning." We are a result of
our own pasts. Knowledge is also a product of the
past, but thought alone is now inadequate to solve
our problems. We can't do it just with our heads.
Consciousness of a greater whole is necessary now—
awareness of ourselves so that we can come into
balance with our own perfectly balanced universe.

Science itself now says it cannot separate the reality of the environment from the reality of our experi-

ence; in fact, that there is no such thing as separateness from anything. If we create that separateness we destroy ourselves *and* our environment.

To me that says, we have to make it together. The chain of the human race is only as strong as its weakest link. Therefore, it is incumbent upon each individual to learn and understand himself or herself by raising his or her conscious awareness. As a *first* step. Resistance to awareness only creates more chaos, and chaos is against natural law, against the glorious balance of the universe. Why do we want to fight the universe?

So each of us has a decision to make. Do I make the effort to understand the grand design by harmonizing my own inner design? If I do, then the question is, *how*?

And the answer is, not easily. If we really want to get right with ourselves and right with the world, we must be prepared to *work* at it, to be wide open with our minds, patient with our understanding, kind to our bodies, and infinitely loving in our hearts.

As I realized when I began: there is so much to learn.

I have tried to share with you some of the things I've learned (and am still learning) and some of the methods that help me "go within." In continuing to read this book, I suggest that you don't do it all at one time. Let yourself become accustomed to the new concepts. In fact, I hope you will stop and give yourself time to assimilate by rereading. Practice the

meditations—and again, do it little by little. Let yourself feel deserving of relaxation, deserving of freedom
from stress. If a lot of the information is too new to
you, or too difficult to absorb, let it alone for a while.
You can always go back and make another attempt at
understanding when your personal exploration has
progressed.

With all I have done in my life I have come to the
conclusion that the most important journey I have
taken is the one into myself. Or, as Yeats said, "It is
not the most important journey, it is the *only* journey."

3

Dealing with the "Reality" of Stress

*A moment's insight can often be worth
a life's experience.*

One of the immediate results at each seminar, and particularly following the talk about the New Age, was always a spate of questions having to do with real problems with which various individuals were trying to cope.

Rather than retelling each and every question (which, in any case, would not be within the compass of a single book), let me try to describe more generalized situations, but using, as I must, myself as a prime example of how things can go wrong—and right.

I have come to realize that "reality" is basically that which each of us perceives it to be. That is, what may be real to me is not necessarily real to a friend, much less a stranger. We each live in a separate world of reality.

I know how abstract and esoteric that sounds, but it is the single most important truth I have learned.

And it has helped me immeasurably in reducing anxiety and stress in my life.

I function in a profession where stress and anxiety are often considered necessary to good work and creativity. Furthermore, the *goal* is the high priority, not the process by which one achieves that goal. What shows and wins is what matters. The end, then, comes to justify the means, and as long as the priority objective is accomplished, God is in his heaven and all is right with the world.

In the meantime, the joy of interaction on a human level is usually sacrificed to the demands of time and money, and the act of stopping to smell the roses is nearly unheard of—unless the roses are part of the deal.

Nor is my particular profession different from many, many others. Goal achievement is the name of the game.

Even now, in many ways, I'm still goal oriented—the conditioning has been long, going back to well before my professional life. But I *am* learning to say no to something that means success at the price of inner peace. I am learning to alter my perceptions and therefore change my "reality."

I arrived at this point of view after years of participating in movie making and stage work as though they were the Normandy Invasion. I finally asked myself, "Where is the war?" Pressure and stress were no longer creative for me—on the contrary, I was beginning to notice that the harmony that resulted when professionals worked well and lovingly together was potentially far more creative than combustible pressure and "motivating" hysteria.

I arrived at the same point of view in relation to friends, family, and fun. With each personal drama I began to see that stress wasn't necessary if I chose not to allow myself to experience it. The script changed if *I* changed my perspective on the "scenes" around me. The *reality* of the scenes themselves shifted as I shifted my outlook on what I was observing. I found that no matter what unpleasantness I found myself involved with, if I stopped and asked myself, "Why have *I* created this? What am *I* learning from this?" the circumstance became not a tragedy but an enlightening experience.

This was not easy when a mugger lunged at me on First Avenue with the clear intention of doing whatever he deemed necessary to get my handbag. I remember my flash reaction that I, by God, did not like playing the part of a victim. Instinctively I changed my "part" and lunged back at him, shrieking like the Wicked Witch of the West until the mugger thought *my* insanity was something he didn't want to tangle with. I changed the script.

I began then to view almost anything negative as a question of *my* point of view, which I could alter. I watched myself as closely as though I were a character in my own play. Then I'd ask myself, "What am I learning about me?" When a producer would renege on a promise, or a director would humiliate me or someone else in front of the crew, or when an airline would lose my luggage, or a cabdriver was rude, or a friend or a lover did something that really hurt my feelings, I would ask myself what I was learning from it and wonder if I needed to learn about myself in *that* fashion any longer. I found that when *I* took the responsibility for what happened to me and claimed the power to have created such a circumstance in the first place, I could then give it up. To continue to blame someone whom I considered to be a culprit was to abdicate my own power. I was, on some level, drawing the unpleasantness to me, participating fully in the throes of the conflict, and, more than anything else, creating the environment for it to happen so that I could learn more about myself.

When I began to experiment with this shift in perception, a new world of positive attitudes began for me. It was as though I was constantly opening up windows onto new landscapes.

I first noticed the phenomenon with a friend of mine who was sick. I felt helpless in trying to help her. I didn't approve of the drugs she was taking. I felt she was giving up and had adopted a negative attitude toward life and her situation. I became despondent about her future. Then it occurred to me that maybe I had created her in my life for a reason. What was I learning from that then? Why did I need her to play such a part in my play? Was she a mirror for me? Was she going through an experience that I did not want to go through myself? Was I observing her as though I were observing myself?

Suddenly the depth of such a new perspective hit me, and as I absorbed the truth of it, I began to work into a system of thought in which I pictured myself releasing her from her pain because *I* didn't want it anymore. In one month, she was better and off the painkilling drugs.

Maybe it was coincidence. Maybe not. I do know that as soon as I allowed myself to take responsibility for my depression about her, *she* began to take responsibility for her healing. I'm still not sure how it works, but I believe it does.

Another time I was involved in a lawsuit with a person who was unreasonably demanding money from me. I became very self-righteous and decided to fight it all the way to the Supreme Court. I was outraged. My lawyers recommended that I settle. I refused, saying the whole thing was grossly unfair. They agreed but said I should pay the money and forget about it. I lay awake nights, fuming, running endless dialogues in which I justifiably devastated this person, playing out scenes in courtrooms with the whole world watching while I reduced him to ruins, which I thought was fair under the circumstances. Internal anger doing its ugly thing to *me*. Then one afternoon in the court chambers I stood off from myself and tried to use my "new perspective" technique. I consciously decided to perceive this man who was demanding money from me as a "teacher." I thought,

"This person is serving as a catalyst for *my* growth. I am being afforded the opportunity here to look at my own anger and study why it is so intense."

Almost involuntarily I dissolved into tears. Slowly the frustration subsided and I realized that it had been there a long, long time. It was not just the result of this immediate situation. Then I *really* cried, relieved that the conflict was gone, grateful that this man had acted as a teacher and a motivator for my evolvement. As a matter of fact, I went even further. I *decided* to see him as a person who had interrupted his own growth to serve as a catalyst for mine. The effect of such a shift in perspective was immediate.

First, when I stopped crying, I instructed my attorneys to pay what he had demanded. To my astonishment, they came back later and said they couldn't understand why, but he had withdrawn his gargantuan claim and now wanted a modest sum. I had never spoken directly to him, but the shift in my attitude somehow neutralized the energy creating the conflict between us. In giving up the battle, or "surrendering my anger," the fundamental energy in the polarity between us shifted until tugging and war were not possible. In the most personal way I realized it does indeed take two to tango, and when I checked out of the dance, the music stopped too.

Again, I don't know how it works, but when sincerely undertaken, this attitude in perspective becomes very powerful. If there is a tug-of-war and one side ceases to pull, the other side collapses because the game depends upon the polarity of opposites. I was learning that to assure a positive and fresh outlook, it was necessary to release the feelings that gave me pain. Not to control those feelings, but actually to let them go. But first came the need to recognize that *it was my choice* to have had those feelings in the first place.

In dealing with the realities of the world we live in I was always drawn to participate in social change. I have enjoyed it, reveled in the successes, and agonized over the delays in moving faster. I worked for peace organizations. I protested against war organizations. I traveled to learn about foreign cultures and customs. I became a feminist. I championed the downtrodden. I worried about the Supreme Court and campaigned for Presidential candidates who respected the liberal persuasion of the intellect. I hung out with journalists and tried to learn to ask questions as rigorously as they did. I observed the press as watchdogs of the government and I deplored the dishonesty and corruption of both. I believed and still do that the American people are hardworking, fair, reasonably honest, and reasonably open-minded; and that a large percentage of them strive to understand the fairness, complications, and intricacies of democracy. We Americans also put up with intense stress. Perhaps the freedom of democracy itself results in stress because it creates the complications of free choices, responsibilities, and competitiveness, which are experienced to a much lesser extent in authoritarian cultures and in societies heavily dominated by religion. The price we pay for a society of free social individuals, versus a society controlled by state or church, is complexity. This causes stress in the individual as well as in the culture itself.

Somewhere along the line, I began to evaluate the speed of my personal growth, relative to stress, to the speed of the growth of the society around me. And I realized, eventually, that if I truly desired social transformation, I would have to begin with the transformation of myself. As with everything else, positive effort has to begin with the self.

I felt that I myself and the society in which I live were suffering, individually and collectively, from the bereavement of something we could not define. For me it was nothing physical or even mental. It was more subtle; more subtle and yet more profound. The bereavement spoke to the spirit of the individual, and thence to the spirit of the nation and its institutions. On some level, we knew intuitively that we had become spiritually impoverished.

In the main, the various churches were not fulfilling our spiritual needs. Besides that, their leadership, in part, was corrupt. I had given up allegiance to formal religion years ago although I continued to try to act with "Christian" love. What other formalized values did we live by? In the world of business, even stock market institutions seemed corrupt, with brokers and big money speculators being slapped on the wrist by inadequate regulations set up by a government that was itself broke and conflicted, lashing about in confusion and waging illegal wars that had become a higher priority than the Constitution.

Along with all of that, we were faced with the omnipresent threat of nuclear annihilation, destruction of the Earth's environment, pollution, the greenhouse effect, a tear in the ozone: a general malaise about nearly everything was being expressed by waves of violent crime, endemic drug use, child abuse, battering of wives, and acts of unprecedented individual outrage. As a democracy, for many years we Americans looked to the authorities *we* had elected and set up for validation and protection of our personal values, ideologies, and identities. Now those institutions, for which we had more regard than ourselves, were disintegrating before our very eyes. Our world, our standards, even our beliefs, appeared to be going to hell in a handbasket.

We were left with no recourse but *ourselves;* we had to look to our own sense of decency and honesty, to our own values—in short, we had to find ourselves within.

Perhaps all of it, the whole mess, was to the good.

Perhaps we created the exterior we are now experiencing with the values and the visions we basically perceive in ourselves. If *we* feel that it is okay to be a little bit dishonest, do a little cheating here, get away with a "smart" little hassle there, what would prevent us from creating powerful institutions that, because of their very power, are a whole lot more than a "little" dishonest—which are, in fact, corrupt. They would merely be reflections of ourselves on a larger scale. We *are* those institutions, after all. We accept what our conditioning has taught us is acceptable.

But if, one fine day, an individual gains new insight into himself, he sees the world around him in a new light also, and as a result he can be more effective in promulgating change. The petty corruption is then no more acceptable than the grand larceny. The changes effected in society would then be a natural extension of the changes of perception in oneself.

I came to recognize the need for personal transformation before I could address any longer the issue of participating in transforming the world I live in. So I began my personal transformation in earnest—some would say too earnest. That doesn't mean that I cut myself off from political and social activism, but it does mean that I saw the necessity for change in a clearer light because I was viewing myself more clearly.

It was at that point that I began a program of exercises of the mind which I put myself through nearly every day in order to accomplish a feeling of inner transformation. As a result, I began to feel more centered in my own power and more aligned, not only with my own destiny but with the destinies of those around me who moved in and out of my life as they pursued their own journeys toward understanding.

At the same time, I recognized how little I knew and understood. When that happened, I tried to focus on what I did know. What I understand today is a result of the knowledge I've gleaned from ancient teachers and modern students who are far more evolved than I. They have all been through their own personal fires in an attempt to understand themselves and how they fit into the great overall universal consciousness of which we are all a part. Whenever things go wrong I have learned to use these events as catalysts to help me understand how I participated in them. In that respect it is *because* of conflicts and problems and pressures that I have learned to handle both them and myself in a more balanced way. So, though the journey within has often been painful, it has reflected every area of the human condition and how I relate to my immediate world. It has helped me in the most practical ways to deal with reality.

I feel a great acceleration in learning taking place all over the world. And God knows the problems are becoming more and more painful. I feel the lessons in my own life, in my relationships, and in my own personal karma. Karma is the law of cause and effect— that which we put out comes back to us. What goes around comes around. Three years ago, it took three months for something I did or said about someone to come back to me. Now I see it return in three hours! What a lesson Karma has become. What an instant and constant reminder that to express with love is to receive love. To express with anger and hostility is to receive the same. The amount of experience in one twelve-hour day is becoming more and more intense, as though I am living three days of experience in one day.

My interpersonal relationships have become deeper and more demanding of honesty and directness. Sometimes it is almost beyond my capacity to feel safe in the increasing demand for sincerity. Sometimes it is very painful to see myself reflected in my friends, loved ones, and—more important—in *my adversaries*. Sometimes it is as though they are each mirroring aspects of myself that I would otherwise be unwilling to confront, and that is the reason these people exist in my life.

I am shifting from my feelings of helplessness about having any effect in helping to change the world, to a position that recognizes there *is* a power within me, and within each of us, so awesome that, when tapped, a transformation in the world could result. It is not only possible but necessary—and part of the next stage of our own evolution and development is to realize (literally "make real") that power. I am obviously not the only one conscious of this approach to bringing about change.

A great awakening is taking place. Individuals all across the world are tapping in to their internal power to understand who they are and using that knowledge to elevate their lives and their circumstances to a higher octave of happiness and productivity. Sharing the search, and the techniques of searching, is only a part of the help we can give one another.

As I have said, this book is an attempt to share how I learned to access the spirituality in myself. Spiritual engineering has become a fascinating study, essential to me in stress reduction and social and personal conflicts.

As I began to go within myself more deeply, and my spiritual studies and investigations advanced, I became more and more interested in the correlation between body and spirit. I had been trained as a dancer so my approach to many of these issues was from a physical culturist's point of view. Anyone who is intensely involved with the physicality of performance knows that the body does not perform well if the spirit is gloomy. Therefore, the connection between the two needs improvement and the access to "interior light" is necessary.

I had heard a great deal about meditation from many of my friends around the world who had been doing it for years, claiming that their very survival depended upon it. "One needs to go within for concentration, balance, strength, and flexibility," they said. "You just can't get that on the outside." So I became interested in the "going within" process. In order to achieve a better and less painful physical performance, I tried my own brand of meditation. I wanted the outer results of my physical life to improve, so that meant I would have to touch the "inner results." I found the experience phenomenal.

One night, after dancing two shows on fifty-odd-year-old legs, Vita-Bath therapy and massage were not enough. In the stillness of my bedroom, I sat cross-legged on the floor and shut my eyes. I got up and put a cassette of music on the tape recorder, sat down, and shut my eyes again. I listened to a quiet tinkle of harp music and tried to allow my mind to have no thoughts at all. This wasn't easy. It required trust and a kind of passive discipline that I was not used to because I am an overachiever who is motivated by will and by thought: but thoughts were what were causing the emotional glitches that in turn manifested as pain and tension in my body.

Then I tried directing my thoughts to my body, beginning with my feet, to relax. Slowly and with care and attention, I told each area of my body to drop its tensions: "Knees, thighs, abdomen, chest, neck, and head, drop your tension!" I knew that each area carried tension for its own reasons. I concentrated on each muscle, flexed and relaxed it, waiting between each new relaxation to make sure the tension was not returning. I allowed the tensions to drift away. And waited, consciously enjoying the growing relaxation. Then slowly I allowed myself to drift away. I drifted and floated . . . drifted and floated. If a thought bothered me, I told it to go away or evaded it by concentrating on a small muscle in a toe or finger. Slowly I realized that my body was completely relaxed. Then I shifted my focus to my interior center. It was easier than I had suspected. I found a ball of light that I'd heard was always there. It was small. I don't know whether I "found" it or whether I visualized it. It was irrelevant. It was there. At first it was barely recognizable in the "darkness" within. So I visualized it until it became larger. Now it glowed. Again I wasn't certain whether it was actually there or whether it was my creation. Again it didn't matter. Slowly I visualized the light growing, becoming a larger and larger ball of pulsating brilliance. Then, when I felt ready, I directed the light to the pain in my back. It was as though I could feel, on another level of reality, the warmth of the light. I held it as long as I could, and my back pain subsided somewhat. I moved on to my legs, particularly my knees, which took a pounding from the high heels I danced in. I visualized the ball of light splitting into two balls, one for each knee. I bathed my knees in the light. I *literally* felt warmth, because I believed in my visualization. I held the two balls of light firmly in my mind. They were real to me because I wanted them to be real. I *perceived* them as real. It was my choice, my power to hold such a reality. I went with it even further. I decided to make the balls of light blue—a brilliant royal blue. I had read that blue was a healing color. Not only did the balls of light become royal blue, but they seemed to be speaking to me as though grateful to be recognized at last! The blue lights melted into my knees. It was as though I was listening to the internal language of color and light, which had a meaning all its own. Yet, I was listening to something I had created. Or had I? Had it always been there inside me, waiting to be recognized as a healing device had I only been conscious of it?

I answered my own question. I had created everything myself. I had created the pain. And I had created the healing. I was in control of it all. The pain *and* the healing were inventions of mine. On some level I didn't understand yet, my knees felt healed. So did my back. I had read about people using visualizations in hospitals (with the aid of doctors) to help heal cancer, tumors, and so on. One boy had apparently healed a hole in his heart by visualizing golden threads sewing it shut. Using some unseen talent and understanding from some other dimensional truth, I had used my own unrecognized power to heal my tired, tense body. If I had created the pain and the healing in my body, was I also creating the pain and the healing in every area of my life? And was that light inside me a tool with which I could create my reality to be whatever I desired?

This, then, was a spiritual technology worthy of examination. This was a new Soul Physics. And how did it happen?

Simply by going within.

4

*Meditate
and Ye Shall Find*

Prayer is speaking to God.
Meditation is listening to God.

Trust tranquility.

So my first tool, or exercise, in my self-exploration became meditation.

The first time my journalist friends and eloquently cynical acquaintances learned that I was "into" meditation, they looked at me blankly and murmured a few vague responses—"Oh." "Really?" "Uh-huh."—and quickly changed the subject. A few said, "Oh, *great!*" and then we were off to what might be a fruitful discussion. The ones I really liked looked me in the eye and said, "Shirl, what the hell *is* meditation? I mean, what do you *do* when you meditate?"

So first, exactly what is it? Put in its simplest terms, for me meditation is the process of relaxing my body and mind so that I can quietly go within myself.

For this to happen, I need to be in a quiet place (at least at first; in the beginning I could rarely meditate in, say, a crowded airline terminal). Meditative techniques vary, but quiet, concentration, and comfort are three keys to settling body and mind.

What does it do? Meditation, or "calm centeredness," allows the mind to recognize other aspects of its identity. Suppression of the mind is not the object of meditation. Instead, the object is to still and calm the personality in order to allow the mind to freely explore the perimeter of its own consciousness.

What do I do in meditation? First, the position in which I meditate is extremely important to me. You should find your own posture, one that creates the fewest pressure points on your body. Meditating in the lotus position as the Buddhist monks do is not important in the beginning. A painful position is disruptive to meditation and contradicts its purpose. On the other hand, a position that is *too* relaxed will only induce sleep. "The middle way," as the Buddhists say, is what is appropriate, which is "the way free of rigidity and tension but also absent of self-indulgence." So sitting in a chair is fine.

The aim of meditation is to stay alert but relaxed. Sitting upright with my back resting against something is what works best for me. This position gives me a "centered" freedom of energy in the spinal column and allows even, gentle, rhythmic breathing. If I'm sitting in a chair, my feet are grounded flat on the floor and one hand is placed on each leg. I place my hands with the palms up and close my thumb and forefinger because that closes the body-current cycle and directs its energy to continue flowing in a cyclic fashion without loss. I keep my lips and teeth closed gently, which also allows the recycling of energy.

I gently rock back and forth and from side to side to "feel" my center and to make sure that I am comfortable. Then I try to imprint on my body the physical feeling when body and spine are centered, so that I will sit the same way behind the wheel of a car, at the dinner table, in front of the television, or at my desk. It's a sort of Braille method of remembering how to sit. I don't mean that I will meditate during those activities, simply that the position of my body will be infinitely more comfortable and less tense.

After I am positioned I close my eyes and begin to breathe naturally. Then I use my breathing as a point of concentration. Concentration is necessary to meditation because it narrows the focus of awareness from the external world in order to access the focus on the internal. I actually follow the course of each breath as I inhale and exhale; in and out. It is remarkable how concentrating on one's own breathing can enable one to enter a meditative state.

The Eastern philosophies use controlled breathing to induce meditative states because it not only provides the intake of oxygen but also requires the expelling of carbon dioxide.

Westerners generally don't pay much attention to the multilayered role breathing plays in our lives. We take it for granted and are, in the main, completely unaware of the miracle that is actually taking place about fifteen times a minute. But breathing is profoundly related to our physical *and* spiritual well-being.

When we are stressed and tense, our breathing rhythms reflect such a state of mind—erratic, uneven, shallow, breath*less,* and so on. When we are peaceful and relaxed, the breathing rhythm is longer, deeper, more all-nourishing within. When we are depressed, or in moments of high stress, we automatically sigh or hyperventilate as though attempting unconsciously to inhale the "spirit force" and the oxygen that comes with a deep and nourishing breath of fresh air. The body knows, the spirit knows, but the Western mind doesn't pay much attention.

In the Eastern cultures, people are more aware of the effect of breathing on the human being. Therefore, they are more expert in how breathing can influence the mental and spiritual well-being of an individual.

Buddhist monks, observed under laboratory conditions, can alter their states of consciousness by employing various techniques of breathing, which in turn affect the physiology of the body. They can alter their brain waves, heartbeats, and pulse rates by using the power of their own consciousnesses to control and vary their breathing.

We could do the same thing, to a somewhat lesser extent. Sometimes when I find myself angry in a traffic jam, I simply close my eyes for a moment, block out the distractions around me by concentrating on the physical feeling as the air enters my nostrils, and gently inhale. I *feel* the breath and follow it to the innermost part of my chest, hold it there for a bit, then gently exhale. I do it again— then again. If I concentrate on the inhale-exhale rhythm, I am always amazed at how soon my anger dissipates and my energy is restored.

To be more specific about it: learn to inhale to the count of ten seconds and exhale to the count of ten. You begin to feel the miracle of the science of healing through breathing. When you can do ten, expand the count to fifteen, then to twenty and so on. An accomplished yogi can take *three minutes* to inhale one breath and another three minutes to exhale! Try it and see what sophisticated control is involved. You will never take breathing for granted again, and the exercise will help in your meditations.

So, even though we are normally unaware of the automatic miracle of our breathing, it is possible to utilize such a basic "involuntary" act in a more nourishing manner. In any case, good breathing is one of the essentials of meditation.

So now you are seated comfortably, eyes closed, concentrating on your nice, easy breathing, in and out, in and out. Already you are more relaxed, calmer.

With the use of breath during meditation comes the use of sound. In the Eastern cultures a sound used during meditation is called a *mantra*. The use of mantras in the West has also become very popular. A mantra is a phrase chanted, hummed, sung, or even just "heard" as a sound within the mind to stimulate the calmness desired in meditation. It is usually a phrase evoking the name of God. Some people go to gurus to get their own personal mantras. Others try out chanting various phrases until one feels right. I, for example, do a silent mantra with each of my hatha yoga poses. I hold each yoga position for twenty seconds and internally chant, "I am God in Light."

The sound vibrations literally caress certain internal areas of myself that seem to respond to the frequency of the mantra's vibrations.

Chanting has always been believed to be very effective in experiencing "God." Murmuring over a rosary; chanting in a synagogue; repeatedly intoning a prayer in church—all are much the same process. However, all religions seem to agree that the actual naming of the deity in each respective culture gets better results. Chanting seems to be a universally accepted method of removing all thoughts and interferences from the mind, which, when emptied, can be filled with "God feeling." There is also new scientific research indicating that mantra sounds that rise slowly and are resonant can decrease the heart rate and induce relaxation. After all, we've been singing our babies to sleep for centuries. . . .

I will have much more to say about chanting in the chapter on chakras, but for the moment I would like to backtrack and talk *about* meditation, rather than how to do it. As a process it is vital to your self-exploration, a basic first step from which the rest flows. So it is important both to get it right and to understand its implications.

Meditation is not something to be taken casually. It is a pathway into the center of self. Therefore, it is extremely important to evaluate your image of your self *before* meditating. If a person believes in demons, evil spirits, Satan, and hell, it is possible that those conditions of belief—fear, panic, guilt—could emerge during deep states of meditation. But remember that such beliefs are a *conditioned* response. They have been taught—indeed, drummed in—precisely in order to produce fear and negativity. Remember too that we create our own reality. In the initial stages of meditation, the psychological and religious makeup of one's temperament could be reflected in one's meditative experience. Belief systems suddenly become "truth" and can return to haunt us. When we begin to go within we are stirring up our conditioned belief systems, sometimes painfully shattering a negative image by which we defined ourselves for many years. That can produce a sense of fear which leads us to stay with "the devil we know" rather than go with the angel we don't know. Fear blocks access to the God within.

To begin to think seriously about one's own inner being is the most profound step we can ever take in the process of maturing. It can obviously be painful and can be even more so when we decide to question old assumptions and beliefs. We are all full of hurt, wounds, and scars. The negative baggage we carry around with us can be alleviated by meditation, but it means being prepared to face some ugly truths, and then to have the courage to fly free of them. Flying free means losing the security of familiar landmarks (even negative ones) or habits through which we have kept ourselves structured and limited. Again, the image you know is one you want to hang on to, no matter how miserable, not only because it is safely familiar but because unconsciously you realize it allows you to blame others for what you are. Desiring to be free within oneself is a serious step to take because with it comes complete responsibility for everything we do. Meditation is not an escape or an indulgence. It is an act of inner responsibility. It takes discipline, hard work, time, effort, and patience with self—which I personally find is the hardest patience to sustain.

Perhaps the most difficult aspect of all, though, is the *continuance* of meditation if it becomes depressing, a letdown, or even frightening. What was at first fulfilling for me became a chore. What seemed so easy in the beginning became more full of obstacles than it was worth. My concentration wandered. My body was uncomfortable. I was impatient. The "light" was not there anymore.

When that happened to me it was a warning signal, a natural stopping point for me, telling me to balance my external world with my internal world. It was necessary for me to re-establish and maintain that balance. *Both* aspects of my experience of reality were required. Inner reality strongly affects outer reality. It should not exist as a reality separately and on its own. In fact, the Trappist monk Thomas Merton declared, "Meditation has no point and no reality unless it is firmly rooted in life."

So the basic purpose of your meditation is to nourish and enrich your physical everyday work, your relationships with people, and your life in general by putting you in touch with your own internal power, through recognition of your spiritual strength. During deep meditation an alignment of mind, body, and spirit occurs, placing each aspect of the self into a better condition of well-being.

This is obviously easier said than done. I have found the most trying aspect is to refrain from *judging* whether I'm doing it right. I expected it to be easy at first. Because I *wanted* to go within immediately, it would happen: if I am responsible for creating my own desires, why not? It didn't work that way. Many things got in the way of my desire to meditate—that is to say, *I* spent a lot of time being disappointed over my progress. Distractions occurred with disturbing frequency, and not the least of these distractions was my own mind. I couldn't stop thinking. My mind was a motorized machine out of control. I wasn't thinking; *it* was! The mental associations bounced around in my head. One image would lead to another. Why did I think about that first performance at the age of three when I held the apple? I was wearing a little green costume. Immediately I associated the green with the Indianapolis 500 speed car races, where they don't like anyone to wear green in the stadium because it's considered bad luck. That led me to think of the people who die in those races, which led me to whether they *really* died, which led me to the power of gravity, which led me to Sir Isaac Newton, which led me to books I had read in childhood, which led me to wonder when I had first experienced mystical feelings, which led me to my father and some of our conversations, which led me to my parents' marriage, which led me to my own marriage, which led me to why I was meditating in the first place!

Finally I began to learn just to let my thoughts be. Let them find their own place. I remembered a Zen priest saying that whenever distracting thoughts "invaded" his mind, he made no attempt to cast them away. He simply waited until they left on their own. "Let them follow their course," he said, "and watch dispassionately as you recognize why they are coming to you. The more one struggles with pushing away a thought, the more power we give it." He said that sometimes he would brush a thought aside as though it was not allowed center stage in his mind any longer but was still allowed to be in the light of the sidelines. With this procedure he allowed room on center stage for a new thought or perhaps even the desired "nothingness" of thought.

An ancient Buddhist master once said that in order to meditate well, "one should learn to be intimate with the unfamiliar and distant toward the familiar." Wandering thoughts are a basic problem in meditation as they are with anything on which we want to concentrate.

When intrusive thoughts are bothering me and refuse to go away, I use the device of focusing on a small object—a button, a flower, or (the scoffer's favorite) my navel, whatever, as long as it is small enough to focus on. Others prefer not to think of any particular object, but instead simply direct their concentration on the images or random lights that appear right behind the eyelids, especially if you open and close your eyes a couple of times. "Watching" those gently shifting lights, trying to make one hold still, looking deep into the darkness beyond— all serve the function of leading your mind away from tensions and into a central channel of concentration that is very relaxed yet completely pinpointed. All the time watching the central focus behind the eyelids, think about your breathing and make sure it is relaxed, deep, and even. This concentration of focus eventually calms and frees the mind: the brain is flooded with oxygen from the deep breathing; the inner eye is concentrated on that spot behind the eyelids; other thoughts, other images, other feelings—all gently slip away. You are flowing with the universal current of *now,* unperturbed by anxieties relating to what you have done in the past or what you might do in the future. As a result stress is reduced. Eventually, with repeated meditations, worry becomes foreign to you, and your physical health improves.

Remember also that there are many processes of meditation.

In fact, everyone meditates to some degree, whether they realize it or not. Daydreaming is a kind of meditation. Listening to music is a meditation. Certain kinds of light sleep can be a meditation. For some, walking or running is a meditation. For me, doing my hatha yoga has become a meditation. Whereas I used to do it while watching the evening news, now I respect it more and use the physical postures of yoga (which means union of mind, body, and spirit plus strength, balance, and flexibility) to calm my mind while I align with body and spirit. I find that I need a notebook and pencil beside me because I have such inspired ideas as a result of this type of meditation—and I don't want to forget them!

Sometimes forgotten phone calls, or letters I should have written months before, come up for me as a reminder when I'm in my yoga meditation. However, even though yoga, mountain climbing, dancing, and athletics are forms of meditation, they are really more of a procedure for putting the body in alignment with mind and spirit. Since meditation includes the *quiet* use of the body while the mind explores itself, a higher level of attunement can occur if the body is not engaged in a highly active occupation.

Again, the object of meditation is to conduct a dialogue with the highest source of our faculties and hence tie in to the universal sources of strength. Calming the body and the mind helps us to connect to the answers that await our questions.

So meditate. I have found that it is best to do it at the same time every day. Your body, mind, and spirit will actually anticipate the scheduled time when the alignment with the Universal Energies takes place. And bear with any difficulties you may encounter, for you will eventually be rewarding yourself from a source that is literally unlimited and to which you are making an important contribution. You will find that you are more than you realized.

With calm, single-minded, relaxed concentration, you come to the core of your meditation. You are going to have an encounter of a very personal kind, with your Higher Self.

5

Superconsciousness and the Higher Self

We are all part of God, and God is part of us.
Nothing can come between us and God.
We are one.

The Higher Self is exactly what the words imply—the best positive elements of your own being, the most reassuring aspect of your own inner strength, your personal expression of the Divine in you. It links you with everything else that exists: it is your channel to the enormous resources of the human potential.

Your Higher Self is of paramount importance in your meditational dialogues. Many, if not most, people find it difficult to tackle problems, to examine their own failures or mistakes, without an exchange taking place. The Higher Self is the aspect of yourself with which you can have an actual discussion about whatever is troubling you. Your concentration on focus is what frees you to do this. The focus removes you a little, creates a small distance between you and your self, gives you the room to explore from a more objective position. Your Higher Self can provide the perspective you need to make fresh assessments of situations, relationships, and your self.

When you are connected to your Higher Self, you are aligned with your spiritual heart center, put in touch with the central source of strength. When you are motivated to proceed from that center, to make decisions, to act, to change, you are functioning in the light. The Higher Self is your personal friend, the guide within, the heart center, the link to your own best real feelings. In listening to it, trusting it completely, and acting on that trust, conflicts can be resolved or simply subside.

To be cut off, or to ignore that heart center, is to intensify conflict, ultimately causing us to be so much out of alignment with ourselves, or out of ease with our God-within, that we become, as the word implies, dis-eased. So many of us don't know about this innate power, or we ignore it or simply find it incredible. Instead, we search for it in our relationships with other people or in our positions in society. What does Joe, or Mack, or Sheila, or the boss, think of us? We are constantly looking for ourselves in other people's eyes. The real question is, What do I think of me? All the time, the only true arbiter, the only referee, the only creator of values has to be the very core of our own being. The Higher Self, the best that is in us, is the real judge of who we are.

So, connecting with your Higher Self is what enables you to see within, and listening to its guidance can provide you with direction in every aspect of your life.

I have found that whatever may be bothering me, whether it's a work-related problem or a trauma in a relationship, I go into meditation and allow my Higher Self to reveal itself to me, and I actually carry on a discussion with it because I know it will never steer me wrong. The way I know that is because its suggestions and ideas are *always* loving. If not, then I haven't connected with my Higher Self; rather, I am connected to my negative ego. Directions coming from the Higher Self are by their very definition attuned to harmonious love and light energy.

Whenever I feel real stress and deep conflict or extreme suffering, I go within myself, into a meditative space, and ask, "What is it I have forgotten about myself?" Meditation is a form of reconnecting with your own inner strengths, of reaffirming who you really are.

When meditation becomes a daily practice, it does not necessarily become easier, but the welcome calm and peace that result from the rituals, from the concentrated focus, become more and more attractive. Meditation becomes an enormous *relief*. The recognition of our higher consciousness becomes more familiar. When we are better acquainted with our higher faculties, they begin to serve us in relation to what we are doing with our lives, and with the larger purpose of our lives, because they link us with our own higher harmony.

Since the Higher Self, the soul, is our personalized reflection of the Divine spark, when we feel love from the heart we are feeling love from our centralized God space. Of course, the Higher Self, the soul, does not inhabit—it *permeates*: it is thought, energy, feeling. It is spirit, and its natural element is ethereal—"of the ethers."

The universal energy of which the Higher Self is a part has always existed, so when the conscious mind "peruses" itself, as it were, it will inevitably touch the soul's experience, which in turn stimulates the memory we have of ourselves, since we, too, are fundamentally eternal spiritual beings. Therefore, self-realization is God-realization. Knowing more of your Higher Self really means knowing more of God. That inner knowledge is radiant with life, light, and love.

Society was transformed by the work of Dr. Sigmund Freud when he explored the possibility of interpreting the subconscious mind. At the end of his life Freud began to question whether there was indeed something beyond even the subconscious mind. He began to explore whether we might have what we now call a superconscious mind, and stated that if he had it all to do over again he would have been a parapsychologist. Freud wondered if this superconscious mind in each of us was attuned to the universal consciousness and if, somehow, it resonated with the harmony of the roles we are all enacting in the Divine Comedy.

When I go within I look for communication and guidance just as in life I sometimes look for advice from good friends. I like to ask questions, check my perceptions as to my opinions, my progress, and in general have a friendly exchange with someone or something which I perceive to be more advanced than "I" perceive myself.

Each of us has personalized our perceptions of whatever we consider reality to be. Each of us has personalized our perception of God and whatever lies within us. In fact, our conception of the reality of this "Kingdom within" can be overwhelming, abstract, and noncommunicative unless we personalize it.

So when we go within and come into alignment with our spiritual power, we come into connection with that spark of Divinity that I have mentioned before, which I call the Higher Self. Some call it the Divine Oversoul, the Divine Center, the God within, the personal interface with God . . . whatever one calls it, it is the personalization of the God Source within us.

When I first made contact with my Higher Self I was aware that I could, from then on, better touch my purpose on Earth and have it fit in with everyone else's. More than that, I became profoundly aware that *everyone* has an important purpose on Earth. I realized more fully than ever that each person alive is having an in-the-body experience of his own for his own reasons, and each person is as important as the other, and each of us is more important than we seem to ourselves.

In fact, I became aware on many levels that we are each an aspect of the great universal intelligence, each playing a profoundly important role in the puzzle of life. Therefore, to recognize everyone equally was part of the secret to putting together my own puzzle a little bit more.

Somehow, I felt on some level that I was important in the scheme of things, and that every single soul was that important, but it was difficult for me to assess myself in such a lofty manner. In fact, I couldn't even say the words which revealed that I myself felt I was tied to a God Source. I felt arrogant, conceited, and undeserving if I said, "I am connected to God, I have God inside of me, I am therefore part of God." I literally looked over my shoulder before I uttered those words aloud. But when I touched and connected with my Higher Self, I suddenly touched the personalized interface with that God Source within, and the experience changed my life.

The Higher Self can be perceived in many different ways. Some people *see* it as a form. Others hear it. Still others sense it so strongly that it communicates with feeling. I usually see and hear it. Mine usually has a human form (a very tall, androgynous being) but sometimes it is only a voice. People have viewed their Higher Selves as persons, animals, shapes of light, geometric designs, and so on. I know one person whose connection with the Higher Self was the most moving experience of his life and it came in the form of a beautiful white feather! Whatever it might reveal itself as, it has no difficulty expressing itself with its God Source understanding, because the Higher Self is our link and reflection to the God energy: it is harmonious, beautiful, peaceful, and commanding. When the connection occurs, the resulting inner calm can be felt physically. You *know* you can trust it. You *know* it is your inner guide, which you always intuitively understood was there but felt too silly to trust. When you finally align with that Higher Self, you have found the guiding light and friend who has always been with you—that guide who has loved you unconditionally through eternity and understands you totally. Since it is reflecting the harmony of the Source, it is happy, loving, and peaceful. A skeptic might call this maudlin and sentimental. To them I say: perhaps it is worth being maudlin and sentimental to some people in order to create better lives, more loving relationships, successful and meaningful work to do, and a peaceful world to live in.

The miracle of it is that the Higher Self is always present and open to recognition whether we recognize it or not. It is our conscious mind that isn't always aware of its spiritual resource. Once again, we are what we are aware of. As we open and expand our conscious awareness, we become more expanded and open human beings. To be close-minded is to limit the consciousness. To limit the consciousness is to limit our potential as an ever-expanding and ex-pressing spark of the God Source.

We begin by aligning ourselves with the God en-ergy of our Higher Selves within us. Again, any change externally begins with a change internally. When the conscious mind becomes aware of the Higher Self, a quickening occurs. That quickening is felt not only in the conscious mind, but also in the body. The quickening is rejuvenative, just as it is when we are inspired, or have a good idea, or we feel love. It is a quickening because we are in touch with a bottomless well of spiritual positivity. It is non-physical, yet it affects us physically. It is beyond the physical, yet we know it's there. It is *metaphysical*.

I feel it happening as a kind of humming well-being. The first time I made the connection with my Higher Self, I was overwhelmed with feelings of love. I was working with a spiritual acupuncturist, Chris Griscom from New Mexico. I lay on a table com-pletely relaxed, allowing pictures to unfold in my mind. It was much like watching a series of excerpts from long-forgotten films unspool in the theater of my mind. For a while I thought perhaps I was making everything up—that *I* was creating the pic-tures I was seeing. How or why I would create, for example, a small child (me) to be run over by a horse wagon driven by a man (an actor I once worked with), I didn't know. Each time I questioned the logic of the pictures I was seeing, the picture disappeared. Since my whole purpose was to experience the internality of my own being, I rapidly came to the conclusion that I was wasting time and energy by questioning and doubting and refuting what I was seeing within myself.

So I allowed the pictures to unravel without judgment. After a series of what I can only define as past-life recalls, one rapidly following another, I realized that the internal scenes had slowed down and something akin to a form shrouded in a golden copper hue came into view in the center of my being.

It took my breath away. I said nothing. Yet, at the same time, Chris described exactly what I was seeing inside myself! It was a powerful form, quietly standing in the center of my inner space, looking at me with total love! The figure was very tall, an androgynous being with long arms and the kindest face I had ever seen. The hair was reddish gold and the features aquiline. The figure lifted its arms and welcomed me to recognize it, saying, "I am the real you!" I heard the words inside my heart and I *knew* they were true. Tears spilled down my cheeks as I proceeded to carry on an internal conversation with this being, who told me things about myself I had always wanted to know. I asked questions about people, my marriage, my family (what relation they had had to me previously), what to expect in my professional work, and so on. I know how preposterous this must sound to someone who believes that reality exists only outside of self. But believe me, when you've had your first taste of accessing your own inner reality, it significantly alters your view of yourself and your life forever.

Connecting with my Higher Self changed me. I *knew* then that the winds of change that had been rippling through me so hauntingly had only been clearing the way for me finally to acknowledge that my inner being was tied inextricably to something so grand and glorious and exciting that I would never be fundamentally alone or unhappy again.

One of the great joys of life for me, if not the greatest joy, has been the process of bridging the gap between the physical and my conscious mind and the nonphysical and my superconscious mind, between what my spiritual consciousness feels and senses and what it is able to manifest physically. Connecting with my Higher Self helped bridge that gap. Then I realized that everything I did in a physical dimension began first as an idea in a spiritual dimension.

Coming into alignment with my Higher Self caused an expanded self-awareness in me, which automatically led me to an expanded awareness and a gentler understanding of others. At the same time, touching my Higher Self created a sense of being aligned with the universal spirit, so that I felt a keener understanding of the concept that we are all one.

Bridging this gap may be the most important connection I've made in life because it enables me to feel empowered and to transform my perception of the outside world I have chosen to live in. By expanding my perception of self, I stop feeling so helpless and victimized and realize with full profundity that I can transform anything I want by transforming myself. That transformation begins within.

Every day on some level and in some way I try to remind myself of who I am and where I come from. I remind myself that every single person on the planet possesses a soul and a Higher Self. I try to remind myself that I am truly important to this world and so is every single person I meet. And the most basic reminder of all: dare I believe that I have an all-knowing, intelligent soul energy operating as a Divine guide that is my personal connection to God? And so does everyone else?

Perhaps our very survival depends upon plunging into that truth—the truth that we are part of a universal God energy that permeates all life, and that it is the right of each unique being to claim his or her participation in perpetuating that miracle.

Perhaps so many of us feel plagued and raddled in our personal lives because we are not connected to the energy of our individual Divine superconsciousness (the energy of the Higher Self). The superconsciousness, which is connected to the universal consciousness, is speeding ahead, expanding and growing even as the universe itself is expanding and growing. I can feel it. We can all feel it. Science tells us that space/time itself is expanding and growing. But it all seems to be happening too fast. Because we are not even aware of the connection, we are out of rhythm with the speed of the expansion. Being out of attunement, out of sync, so to speak, causes conflict and chaos. If we would open our conscious minds to the existence of the Higher Self and the superconsciousness in each of us, we would flow more in attunement with the universal energies that we sense are speeding and expanding beyond us. Because we feel unable to keep pace with that speed, we often feel that the dynamics of our lives are out of our control. When that happens, we feel helpless and unable to cope.

Well, as long as we remain limited in our awareness of the superconsciousness within, our lives will feel out of control, because the expanding universe and even time itself will continue to speed ahead whether we are capable of keeping up or not.

The intensity of experience itself is speeding up for all of us. What used to take several months to come to a head erupts now in a few days. Our emotional learning experiences are occurring at a rate that sometimes puts us into a swirl of futility. Many people don't even see a negative occurrence as a learning experience at all because they haven't been exposed to such a concept. Instead, they continue to feel victimized and helpless, ultimately blaming others for what they drew to themselves in order to learn—however unaware they may be of that fact.

I believe such negativity can be remedied by going

within to recognize and appreciate *self*. There is an urgent need for people to recognize the power within themselves, to know themselves as a spark of God. Everyone basically knows why they're here, what lessons they're learning. Everyone basically knows why they chose their husbands, their wives, their jobs, their bosses. They know why they've chosen the city and the country they live in. Somewhere, if they listen carefully enough to the answers of the Higher Self, they'll hear the truth of why they've chosen the life they are leading and what they came into this life to accomplish. If they listen, connect, attune, and align, ultimately they will be more enlightened as to who they really are.

No one is alone in this search. People may not talk about it much, but nearly everyone is asking the same question: How do I make the connection with my purpose? Connection is the key—with the Higher Self, with the Earth, with the universal source—with superconsciousness.

6

The New Age and Rational Thought

It is as vital to be physical
as it is to be spiritual.

To find God within oneself it would seem necessary at least to acknowledge his existence. The knotty question of whether God exists, and if so, where, points up a basic difference between Eastern and Western systems of consciousness. The Eastern search for God is directed within the individual; the Western search, without. The Eastern sage believes God is within and integral to human existence. The consciousness of Western religion says God is separate from man, superior to him, and that the deity's existence must be accepted on faith.

But now we have an astounding and marvelous thing happening. Science, which traditionally has had to maintain a position of "no proof, hence no God" (and no one is more hidebound than your average scientist), now finds itself in the rather delicate condition of having to admit that, yes, there *is* something, neither energy nor matter, but *some*thing whose existence we have proved but which we cannot really measure, or weigh, or see. Because if we try to observe it, it changes. If we even think about it, it changes! And this non-energy, non-matter, non-solid something is the stuff of which the universe is made. What a dilemma! Because nobody has yet figured out how this chameleon "something" has the knowledge to make itself into a planet or a poodle.

The Eastern system of thought tends toward going within for the answer. It is right-brained: intuitive, open, capable of holding contradictory concepts without confusion. The traditional Western system of thinking is more left-brained: linear, logical, and rational.

New Age thinking is an attempt to balance the two by pressing past the linear thinking of the rational to include the depth and dimension of the intuitive. I have found that meditation and the solitude of going within opens up my internal universe, whereupon my previous concepts of time, of life and death, of God himself seem quite limited. It is a liberating and adventurous experience.

Similarly, from the scientific books I have been reading, I've learned that the field of subatomic quantum physics has opened up a whole new world for modern scientists to explore. Michael Talbot's masterly work *Beyond the Quantum* is a particularly clear and fascinating presentation of complex theories and experiments of several New Age scientists. Some of their conclusions have given rise to speculation about the "realness" of reality and highly controversial views (in scientific circles at least) on what can only be described as mysticism. Science and spirituality seem to be converging. Alain Aspect, for instance, in his 1982 experiment, proved that at least one of two conclusions had to be true—either reality as we define it does not exist, i.e., *we* create reality to be what we think it is, *or* communication with the past *and with our future* does exist.

Rupert Sheldrake, a biochemist, has postulated a superimposed *field* (web of information) which he calls a "morphogenetic field", or M-field, to account for the conveyance of information within like species. He calls this informational movement "morphic resonance." On an experimental basis his theory gains support from a thirty-four-year study by William McDougall in which rats from totally different, widely separated genetic lines, nevertheless learned the new useful habits that only one group was working with—except that "learn" is slightly misleading as this information appears to have become universally available once a certain number of rats had acquired it. In other words, the information had entered the rat M-field.

Again, there is the famous "hundredth monkey effect"—not really a controlled experiment, but an observed event that occurred in the 1950's on the island of Koshima. Researchers performing various studies of the local population of monkeys dumped sweet potatoes on the beach. This particular species of monkey had never encountered sweet potatoes before, and while they liked the vegetable they clearly did not like its sandy coating. Then one monkey genius discovered she could clean the potatoes by washing them in the sea. First a few other monkeys, observing this, did the same, later followed by several more busy potato washers. Then quite suddenly, all at once, the entire troop took to washing their potatoes. At this point, other researchers, *on islands far removed from the original,* reported that all *their* monkeys started to *utilize the same washing technique!*

The conclusion is that information acquired by a certain number of any given species acts like a flashpoint—from that point forward the species as a whole is equipped with that information. The new knowledge has entered their M-field via morphic resonance. Moreover, since the species can be widely separated geographically but all its descendants everywhere will also be born with that information, when Sheldrake talks about an M-field he is talking about a subatomic informational web that operates across both space and time. In addition, the M-field may well be connected to the subatomic particle behavior that always expresses itself as a movement toward *wholeness,* a movement that is true for all forms and species, including crystals. . . . And, in further addition, the M-field may account for the ability of undifferentiated cells to decide which ones will grow into a hand, or a head, or whatever; or, when a group of generalized cells is divided in half, to create twins—that is, two *wholes*.

And as recently as 1984, Nobel Prize-winning neurophysiologist Sir John Eccles announced the discovery of what he believes to be biochemical evidence supporting the existence of the human soul.

Perhaps I should take back my remark about "hidebound scientists." . . .

Many, many men and women in the worlds of science are now opening their minds to new ways of thinking. In the past ten years, extraordinary experimentation has shattered long-held beliefs and opened up whole new areas for exploration and speculation. Science still shies away from words like *God* and *soul* (despite Sir John), using more comfortable phraseology such as *information,* or even *universal information bank* (scientists do not, of course, acknowledge any coincidence between this concept and the system of information known as "Akashic Records" in the East). What is happening, in fact, is that Eastern mysticism, which intuitively accepts so much, and Western pragmatism, which insists on scientifically proving so much, are coming together. In my opinion, this New Age is the time when the intuitive beliefs of the East and the scientific thinking of the West could meet and join—the twain wed at last. For me, both are necessary, and both are desirable.

With this understanding I can more easily appreciate how people (including myself) can remember past existences and "clairvoyantly" see future times.

I found in my travels that such experiences are well accepted in the East, while here at home in the West these ideas still disturb our linear concepts of rationality. But rationality itself is a tenuous concept. We "stack" information to conform to our reality—that is, we see what we want to see, influenced by what we already know. The question of reality then becomes a question of perception, conditioning, and beliefs.

How to sort out the multilayered levels of belief and perception is what is motivating new approaches to truth in science.

Basic to New Age subatomic discoveries is the concept that in the subatomic world—the stuff of the universe—everything, every last thing, is linked. The universe is a gigantic, multidimensional web of influences, or information, light particles, energy patterns, and electromagnetic "fields of reality." Everything it is, everything we are, everything we do, is linked to everything else. There is no separateness.

This understanding brings us to the most controversial concept of the New Age philosophy: the belief that God lies within, and therefore *we* are each part of God. Since there is no separateness, we are each Godlike, and God is in each of us. We experience God and God experiences through us. We are literally made up of God energy, therefore we can create whatever we want in life because we are each co-creating with the energy of God—the energy that makes the universe itself.

Science itself is attempting to establish, in the exploration of subatomic-particle behavior, whether mankind is creating its own reality with the God Source energy, or with *some* form of universal energy of "information." Life itself is a creation from this energy. What is it, then? If the pattern of that energy has order, and balance, and grace (which science claims it does), if it has meaning in terms of all life, what is to distinguish it from what the New Age calls God?

In my reading on the relationship between mysticism and quantum physics I was fascinated to learn that each organ of the human body has a harmonious energy pattern that science can now identify. The organs are matter within an electromagnetic energy field, which William Burr described as "the blueprint for life." In the spatial relationship between the molecules in that energy field, the molecules are, relatively speaking, farther apart than the planets in our perceived universe are to each other. The universe within, then, is more vast than the universe without! Furthermore, according to science the solidity of matter is actually an illusion. The grand illusion, as a matter of fact, is that our physical world is solid. It is not. It is a molecular structure of subatomic particles that *appears* to be solid. Is this science or is this mysticism?

Science says there are three basic components to the event of an experience: time, space, and matter. When there is a consensus that each of those component parts exists, we have what we term reality. So it only takes an agreement of perception for anything to exist as real. According to science, the physical dimension becomes real only through the consciousness of our intentions. Reality is then actually an intention that becomes an illusion of consciousness.

The molecules that create the illusion of physical reality are organized by electromagnetic fields of energy. If through our "intentional consciousness" we alter the frequency of those electromagnetic fields, we "defy" (or alter) reality. Examples of that are feats by yogis who stop their heartbeats by will (i.e., intention of consciousness), fire-walking, levitation (reversing the polarities of the body relating to gravity), and so on.

So each of us is a living, walking electrical field of energy. Our field of energy organizes the molecular structure that we *perceive,* both within and without, as physical reality.

One of the most extraordinary and beautiful truths about subatomic worlds is that they tend to "move" toward order. Each of us is an amalgamation of frequencies that *needs* to be harmonious and compatible, whose natural order is to move toward harmony. This harmony, this order, is impeded and distorted by feelings of fear, anger, hatred, et cetera. Here, right here, is the interface between who we think we are and the subatomic world from which we have created ourselves.

Conscious awareness of these dynamics within can

help to bring our frequencies into balance. When that occurs, "reality" itself goes beyond our customary comprehension of it—the form of reality takes on a dimension we do not normally perceive.

Highly self-realized and disciplined people with total self-awareness can create antibodies that cure disease. Of course, that is a contradiction in itself because totally self-realized people rarely become diseased. They are in total "easement" within themselves. They will be more, or less, dis-eased depending on the degree of their spiritual awareness. Disease in the body, as I have learned from experience, begins first with a blockage of energy in the spirit. For me, *all* of my physical problems begin in my *con sciousness*. And when I stop to meditate, when I go within and literally "ask" my Higher Self why I am manifesting a particular physical problem, I usually get an answer and always it relates to some fear, rejection, or feeling of "nonworthiness." I try to reconnect with spiritual harmony and God. If I'm successful, I get well. This particular aspect of New Age thinking—self-healing—is a highly developed stage, obviously a long way down the road to full self-awareness.

It requires patience and a full confrontation of one's own consciousness, which can sometimes be extremely painful, because it involves the most difficult of all human feelings: *self*-forgiveness. I have found that I first have to *admit* that I am afraid, or angry, or rejected, or feeling undeserving. *Then* I can forgive myself for allowing myself such disharmony. When I forgive myself, healing begins.

So, since both scientists *and* mystics claim that harmony is the natural order of life, I try continually to remind myself that I have the right and indeed the Divine inheritance to reflect that harmony in myself. It's not easy in a world full of suffering and anger and anguish, but I am learning that if I work on myself to attempt to achieve an internal reality of harmony, it alters my physical reality.

It is now possible to monitor and correlate how a change of consciousness affects physical reality. An individual capable of this is manipulating his or her physical reality by manipulating his own electromagnetic fields of energy. And he does that by consciously orchestrating his patterns of thought. The resulting manifestation of the thought patterns alters the physical reality. Thus, we begin to see how it is possible to create one's own physical reality with the use of thought and higher conscious awareness.

Instrumentation now makes it possible to quantify these phenomena and therefore observe the biological and psychological effects. As a result of these observations, some members of the scientific community are now saying we need to factor in consciousness in our scientific studies. The behavior of that which is being observed is directly altered by the consciousness of the observer. There is no separateness. We each have an inextricable effect on everyone and every thing around and beyond us. Each and every cell in our bodies is reacting to electro-magnetic information from the universe at every moment. *We are all, everything is, connected.*

This was a truly profound understanding for me, particularly in a sociopolitical sense. If our bodies, made up of vibratory patterns, resonate to the "information," or the "field," of the entire subatomic world, and each individual vibratory pattern moves toward harmony, then when we are in touch with that harmony we are more peaceful. Suddenly I could understand how spiritual awareness included relevance to politics and society as a whole. The more aware we made ourselves of our own electromagnetic fields, the more integrity of harmony we would have within ourselves and with the rest of the world in the harmonious universe. The more unaware we remained, the more randomly chaotic our lives would continue to be. Each one of us is different because we each have accumulated different libraries of stored information in our experience. But we can become more aware of our personal libraries with techniques of breathing, meditation, exercise, and visualization. In the solitude of these practices we not only become more in touch with our own accumulated information, but in doing so we can more easily exchange and share with others and their experiences, making it very much simpler to relate to and understand the differences in reality that we each perceive. Thus, we would more readily understand ways to achieve peace with those who perceived reality differently than we do. Spiritual technology and Soul Physics were becoming politically and socially pragmatic to me.

Science now says that the DNA molecule is in effect an antenna and that each coding has its own electromagnetic wavelength. It is believed that the DNA code carries within it racial memories of the collective unconscious and that we create the physical dimension with DNA codes. If this is so, then I can understand why past-life recall is possible. Again, I realize how the Eastern systems of thought have gone within to find the source of our human truth, while the Western systems of thought have pursued the puzzle of origins through the sciences of technology. *Both systems are valid.*

Science makes a set of hypotheses, makes its observations, then experiments to prove or disprove. When there is a large enough consensus on the result, it becomes scientific fact. The Eastern mind would say the scientist is creating what he is observing and therefore what he wants to believe anyway. The Western scientist has to concede that the electromagnetic patterns of his thoughts are a field of energy that directly affects what he is observing.

Each warrior of truth has a separate path. Scientists and mystics are inseparable, though, each motivated by the search for the creator of the grand design of which we are a part and to which each of us is a contributor. For simplicity's sake, some of us call that grand design God.

When I change my consciousness to include myself in that God-creator, I change my external reality. And I find that the more harmonious I am in my spiritual consciousness, the more I can be tolerant of others, peaceful with myself, and capable of allowing myself to feel the natural principles of integration and harmony with everything in creation. If I'm out of alignment with my spiritual nature, nothing much goes well for me and I am unhappy and frustrated to boot.

As soon as I understood the positive logic in accepting the God energy within myself, it didn't seem so blasphemous to me, so outrageously ridiculous to others. My limiting education and narrow systems of thought had actually prevented me from understanding the deeper and more real possibility of harmony and peace. I don't mean to say that now I feel peacefully harmonious all the time. Far from it. But whenever I really get out of balance I look for silence. Silence is necessary to perceive the truth of our God-selves inwardly. We could take the mystery out of mysticism *and* out of technology if we allowed ourselves to find the time and the silence necessary to access that eternal God energy within.

This is not what I would call a "cult of self," nor is it selfish, self-indulgent, self-centered, or self-aggrandizing. It is what I call survival. It is evolution. It is basic pragmatic functionalism. It is necessary to growth, progress, and a more humane technology. It would help us clarify our intent and galvanize our purpose. It would more fully enrich our lives and inspire our work. The more peaceful and happy we are individually, the better work we produce. The more angry, chaotic, and out of touch with ourselves, the more the work reflects that state of mind, that negativity.

And all of it comes down to the belief that we each contain and hold the God-spark within us. Our humanity toward one another directly reflects the humanity we feel for ourselves. And that humanity is directly related to self-love. If God is love and each of us possesses God within us, then all of us would be happier and more peaceful with one another, recognizing that the more we try to *express* as God, the more harmony there will be in the world.

That is the basic principle of the New Age. And science agrees that harmony is the natural order of the universe.

Begin with self; recognize the God within, and the result will be the recognition, with tolerance and love, that everyone else possesses God within as well. In other words, we are each part of God experiencing the adventure of life.

7

A Rainbow
of Expression

What we are
What we experience
What we can be
Is the reflection cast
by the human rainbow.

In the course of my spiritual investigations I learned about a specific power of aligning with certain energies within, which has altered and improved my concept of internal harmony ever since. A consistent and ancient belief held by man down through the ages is that the physical body is but the reflection of a series of more subtle bodies of energy within, and that these subtle bodies of energy reflect the vibration of the God Source. *That* vibration is the vast energy at our disposal if we know how to access it.

The Egyptians, the Chinese, the Greeks, the North American Indian and African tribes, the Incas, the early Christians, the Hindus of India, the Buddhists of Asia, and today's metaphysicists and mystics everywhere in the world share, to some degree, a common belief: that the body is only a physical manifestation of energies that together create an entity beyond that which can be seen only with the naked eye, and that those levels of existence, those energies, that entity, reflect the nature of God and the universe.

The correlation between man and God has been the subject of the most profound of all wonderings. The ancient schools of study focused this correlation on esoteric systems of energy located in seven centers of the human body. These centers are called *chakras,* translated from the Hindi to mean "wheels of energy."

Just as there are seven levels of consciousness, seven ages of man, seven colors in the rainbow color spectrum, and seven notes on the Western musical scale, there are seven primary chakras in the human body. We cannot see the soul or measure the aura of human energy; nor can we measure these centers. But we know they exist.

The chakras represent the subtle anatomy of human beings just as the physical organs represent the gross anatomy. The subtle and the gross are connected. There are seven endocrine glands, which correspond to the seven chakras. Therefore, our bodies (the vehicles through which we express ourselves) reflect the balance or the imbalance of subtle and gross anatomy. As I was learning I was continually reminded that when and if the spiritual is out of kilter, ignored, or misused, it will show up in the physical—*not* the other way around! The physical (gross) is a reflection of the spiritual (subtle).

Western systems of thought, dedicated to "rational"

provability, to the measurement of progress by the wonders of technological development, have lost recognition of the chakra wheels of energy. In fact, I don't know if we were ever aware of them. But the ancient Oriental masters were adept at this spiritual technology. Happily, this knowledge and understanding are finding new recognition in the West. Here is a summary of what I learned in my travels through India, the Far East, and the Himalayas.

According to the masters, the soul creates the body in accordance with the laws of the earth plane, in order to provide a "house" for itself in this physical dimension. The physical body thus gives the soul the opportunity to be focused in time and space. The chakras govern this physical reality because the seven centers of consciousness are the areas through which the human personality experiences itself. The chakras, then, are both a communicative, and a controlling link, connecting the soul entity (the Higher Self), the personality, and the body that the soul has created through which to express itself.

Since this human personality is the medium through which we communicate with one another, recognition of the chakras and the various energies they hold and connect to is essential to an understanding of what human expression in the physical is all about.

It was helpful for me to think of my body as a musical instrument inside of which were seven notes, seven different rates of vibration, and a spectrum of seven colors. If I played only one note or focused on one color all the time, my instrument would be monotonous and boring. But learning to work with all of the notes, colors, and vibrations created a harmonious, kaleidoscopic work of art. I learned I could work with my musical instrument and play harmonious music for myself.

The seven chakras of energy are not in need of opening. They are always open, spinning, and in complete harmony. It is our minds that are closed and don't recognize their harmonious importance and existence. Therefore, we don't work to open the chakras, we work to open the mind to recognize the chakras. That is why the basic steps of meditation are so important.

Our personalities become a product of the recognition allowed by our minds of chakra "language," or energy, and are rich or limited, open or closed, to the degree of that recognition. The more we work with the spiritual dimensions of our beings, the more we are conscious of the chakras, the more attuned and centered as human beings we become. When we attune the conscious mind to the spiritual energies of the chakras, the mind itself begins to expand with an awareness of its own higher consciousness. So it is through the chakras that we fully integrate mind, body, and spirit.

Our physical sciences look to biological and physiological patterns of data as the source of the human personality, but when we align our chakras we are integrating a memory of our soul's experience, which allows our personality to manifest—make visible—the aspects that make it unique. The human personality then emerges as an expression of the soul: the body is merely the vehicle, or temple through which the soul incarnates and expresses itself.

Since the chakras are created with soul energy, when we attune to them we are attuning to the specialized centers that have shaped our characters and our natures each time we have entered the physical plane to learn and experience. The more we are attuned to the unique energies within our bodies, the more we can open our consciousness to the higher resource to which they are connected and of which we, and they, are a part.

The more we are connected to higher resources, the more infinite we become as human beings. Carl G. Jung claimed that the chakras were the gateways of consciousness in man, receptive points for the inflow of energies from the cosmos and the spirit and soul of man; that the chakras are always aligned with the Divine God energy because they are the creation of the soul.

The ancient masters claimed that good health depends upon the correct alignment and functioning of these seven etheric energy centers: that the union of spirit and matter manifests as consciousness in the physical, and the seven chakras govern how our consciousness is experienced in the physical body. How then to open the mind to the energies of the chakras?

In order to understand the meaning of aligning the chakras it is necessary to understand the area of physical consciousness that each one represents.

For me, the seven chakras can best be identified by using key words that represent the emotional issues associated with each chakra. The function of the physical glands associated with the emotional issues of each chakra then becomes clear.

The first chakra, also known as the base chakra or root chakra, is located at the base of the spine and is defined as the chakra that governs one's understanding of the physical dimension. It is the grounding chakra—that is, it grounds one in the Earth, it puts both feet on the ground: it is pragmatic, ultrarealistic, the "survival" chakra responsible for our balance and our attitudes toward fight or flight. It is therefore the chakra that externalizes as the adrenal gland, and it also governs the functioning of the kidneys and the spinal column. It is esoterically perceived as *red*.

Indian Hindu Vedic seers claim that the base chakra also channels the energy of the human will and that the entire human system balances itself on this base support. It is the seat of insecurity, where survival, possessiveness, and materialism lie. It is referred to as the survival chakra because it is through this center that we feel fear or anger when threatened.

These negative aspects to survival lead to an interesting anomaly. Because the root chakra is ground-based, its fundamental nature is secure. But the personality, conditioned by the process of evolution, has learned to fire off alarm signals, triggered by *perceived* threat, so that the adrenals will start pumping adrenaline.

The intriguing thing that explorers have learned about animals living in an environment previously devoid of mankind is that *they do not perceive humans as a threat*. Even now, animals in the wild react to their natural predators only while an actual hunt is in progress. The rest of the time they get along peacefully, allowing quiet coexistence at a respectful distance.

Is it conceivable that when humans first became hunters and eaters of flesh, the glandular tie to the security chakra evolved in a distorted fashion? I wonder how far back we would have to go to learn when people first became afraid of people. This would be an interesting area for exploration as greater skills develop in working with the chakras, and might help to explain some of the basic insecurities that we as individuals may feel.

As I learned how to work with my chakras, it was with this first chakra—the red chakra, the root and base of the human chakra system—that I worked with first. In the meantime, though, I needed to learn where and what the other six chakras were.

The second chakra is the sexual chakra, the chakra of creativity, located in the reproductive organs (the ovaries in the female and the testes in the male). It is the color *orange* and governs one's creative attitudes in relationships, sex, and reproduction.

The third chakra is located in the solar plexus. Its glandular externalization manifests in the pancreas and it governs the action of the liver, stomach, gallbladder, spleen, and certain aspects of the nervous system. This chakra is the clearinghouse for emotional sensitivities and issues of personal power. Its color is seen as *yellow*.

Sensitives often comment that they see most people who have emotional attachments to children and loved ones "leaking" from the third chakra. The yellow color spills out of its center and depletes the energy of the individual experiencing concern, possessiveness, and proprietary interest in the lives of those they love. This does not mean one should not be concerned, for instance, about one's children. But the concern should be in terms of the child's well-being, not for the relief of one's own possessive anxiety.

This third chakra gives all of us more problems than any other because it is essentially the "seat of emotional living." Out of unbalanced emotions come ulcers, digestive problems, and liver, spleen, and pancreatic troubles. The positive and negative energy polarities are located in the solar plexus chakra, which, when balanced, is bi-polar, meaning that the positive (masculine-yang) and negative (female-yin) are perfectly harmonious. When a person crosses his arms in front of his solar plexus, he is blocking off the energy of that potential balance by adopting a defensive posture; or to put it another way, he is protecting his feelings by crossing his arms.

When a person is overwhelmed with emotion there is an automatic triggering of an almost involuntary act called crying. When tears well up, if allowed to proceed, they often lead to sobbing. The physical act of sobbing produces a gentle—or sometimes not so gentle—massage of the solar plexus. The deep and heavy sob caresses the solar plexus, which can then relax, releasing the pent-up emotion that it was unable to process in the first place. "Having a good cry" enables the third, yellow, chakra at the solar plexus center to reestablish its balance and release itself from emotional overload.

If the sobbing doesn't bring this about, sometimes a person will vomit. The act of vomiting activates the diaphragm muscles. The diaphragm itself is a dome-shaped muscle that separates the lower three chakras from the upper four chakras. Vomiting actually clears out the physical manifestation of what is causing the emotional overload. That is why we feel so "spacey" and mellow after a good cry or a purging vomit! It is the body's defense mechanism against feeling more of an emotional overload than it is able to handle.

The fourth chakra is called the heart chakra. Its glandular externalization manifests in the thymus. The fourth chakra governs the heart, blood, and circulatory system. It has a strong influence on the vagus nerve, located in the brain, and also governs the immune and endocrine systems. Its color, usually seen as *green,* depends on the level of clairvoyant perspective from which it is viewed.

When I began meditating on the heart chakra, I soon realized that the key word was *acceptance*— acceptance of others, and acceptance of the love within self. It is often said that when we pray we speak to God. Meditation is when God speaks to us through the God within via the communicative centers of energy. Achieving true meditation on all the chakras is a path to complete inner peace.

The Sanskrit word for the heart center is *anahata*. It means "that which is ever new, that which is self-sustaining." Through the heart chakra we "fall in love." Instinctively, when we recognize the attraction in another we move from the heart chakra down to the yellow solar plexus chakra of emotional integration, to the bright orange sexual chakra, which is motivated by love, and finally to the root chakra, the warm red energy that inspires us to settle down, to ground ourselves in the Earth with this person.

The Eastern mystics say we define our personalities through the heart chakra, which they believe is the core of the soul. The soul manufactures the "forever hormone," which, when experienced, keeps us feeling forever young through love.

The "forever hormone" is said by the masters to emanate as energy from the heart when one is in a state of love. This energy hormone nourishes all of the lower chakras, where we feel insecurity, survival needs, and fear.

It is amusing to me that we never "go (up) in love"—we always "fall (down) in love." To me that is the intuitive recognition of the soul attraction first experienced in the heart chakra, which then spills down through the energy systems of emotion (third chakra) and sexuality (second chakra) until it becomes anchored in the Earth (first chakra).

The fifth chakra is the throat chakra. Its focal point of activity is the thyroid gland and it governs the lungs, the vocal cords, the bronchial apparatus, and metabolism. This chakra is usually seen as *blue*. It is the center not only of expression and communication but of judgment.

I find that it is extremely important to work with the fifth chakra these days because individual self-expression *without* judgment is the task of balancing a free democracy. We feel the urge to tell the truth as we see it. But we should try to accomplish this without judgmental condemnations that hurt others. Again, when we remember that what we perceive in another is a reflection of ourselves, we become less judgmental. So when we freely express harsh judgment of another, we are in effect talking about those aspects of ourselves that trouble *us* the most. I find that when I feel negatively judgmental about someone, by examining that feeling in meditation on the fifth, blue, chakra, I usually achieve better understanding of my own communicative dynamics and better judgment of what to say and what not to say to others.

The sixth chakra is located in the center of the forehead. It is better known as the third eye and externalizes as the pituitary gland. Its color is usually seen as *indigo*—a deep, vibrant color composed of red and blue. Primarily it governs the lower brain and nervous system, the ears, the nose, and the left eye, which is the eye of the personality.

Idealism and imagination center in the sixth chakra, which also reflects inner vision and governs the outer expression of that inner vision. The mystics say that to access a limitless potential of thought it is necessary to "tickle" the pituitary. They accomplish this through visualization in meditation. They focus on the third eye and allow their inner vision to be limitless.

The seventh chakra, or crown chakra, is located at the top of the head. Its color is seen as *violet* or sometimes *white*. It externalizes as the pineal gland and governs the upper brain and right eye. Within the crown chakra are the counterparts of all the other chakras. It is the chakra that speaks, in combination with other chakras, to unlimited consciousness and Divine purpose. It is through this chakra, they say, that one reaches, ultimately, the feeling of integration with God.

The upper three chakras form what is known as the Golden Triangle, which represents a triad of energy reflecting the perfection of cosmic harmony in a balanced way, which then infuses the neurological, or nervous system, within the physical body. A kind of esoteric pumping effect occurs whereby three harmonious cosmic energies are "milked down" through the entire chakra system to the root chakra, which grounds the harmony and thus provides a feeling of security. Thus reinforced, the cosmic energy travels back up the chakra system until it reaches the crown chakra again and the cycle is complete, whole. The energy is, as it were, plugged in, the circuit connected.

Unfortunately, in most of us the return of cosmic energy back up the chakra system is blocked in either the sexual chakra or the solar plexus, in our strong feelings of attraction/deprivation, or love/possession, need/power, et cetera. The problem does not lie in whether or not we are infusing the cosmic energies. We are. But we tend to prevent their completing the circuit of power by allowing them to become stuck in the second and third chakras. Meditating on those chakra energy centers will help free the blockage. The results are often astonishing. Again, we will explore this form of meditative technique more fully later.

When all the chakras are recognized and aligned

with the conscious mind, the consciousness of the individual is expanded and made more aware of the energy sources available for good health and happiness. An imbalance in the chakras (or, more precisely, imbalance in recognition of the chakras) disturbs and blocks the flow of energy within the consciousness and properly functioning physical health becomes distorted.

Meditating on the chakras was extremely important to me, because anything I could learn about how they related to my physical body was helpful in working with these energy centers. In learning how the chakras affected my body, I also learned something about how they contribute to emotional growth and development.

The philosophy surrounding the knowledge of the chakra energy centers included cycles of growth in terms of years. I learned that the development of the physical human body in relation to its soul is divided into cycles of seven. Each cycle deals with the emotional issues of the corresponding chakras.

The first seven years of a human being's life revolve around survival and instincts of adjusting to the physical earth-plane experience. One learns to crawl, walk, run, eat, and accept the physical expression of embracing, being loved and caressed, and so on. We develop our sense of balance until the physical form securely anchors itself to the Earth, according to how effectively these emotional experiences occur, and then prepares for its process of learning—the red, root chakra controls the assimilating of these processes.

In the second seven years (eight to fourteen years of age) sexuality develops and produces crises of various kinds so that the human being can develop the subjective mind, the capacity for creativity and for fuller consciousness of self-identity—sex and identity are controlled through the orange, genital chakra.

The third seven years (adolescence to age twenty-one) deal with issues of emotionality relating to other people, the assessment of personal power, and the practice of free will—all of the problems of adolescence are felt through the yellow, solar plexus chakra.

The fourth seven years (ages twenty-two to twenty-eight) develop a human's relationship to love—self-love and mature love of others—and abilities of evaluation and decision in terms of lifestyle. Through the green, heart chakra the individual decides during these years how harmonious he desires to be in life.

The fifth seven years (ages twenty-nine to thirty-five) are the years when a human questions and/or reaffirms the wisdom of his or her self-expression and is dealing heavily with the consequences of judgment in others. This is the time when we become profoundly aware that how we express ourselves is how we live with others.

In the sixth seven-year period (ages thirty-six to

forty-two) we begin seriously to question our spiritual nature as it relates to the lifestyle we have created. All the knowledge we have gained begins to transmute to a kind of wisdom, and during these years we decide to develop our spiritual nature or we affirm the consequences of avoiding this growth.

In the seventh seven years (ages forty-three to forty-nine, or late forties and fifties) we actively attempt to integrate ourselves with the understanding of God—that is, to bring our exterior and interior lives together into a harmonious whole with the Source. That goes on for the rest of our lives.

We can become emotionally stuck, blocked, or damaged at any point along the line, and/or at differing points with respect to differing aspects of growth. We have all heard, for instance, of the infantilized male, or the child-woman. The task then is to free ourselves from those blockages of consciousness, which will automatically free up the blockages in our physical experience. Again, the body reflects the disorders of the soul.

Body Language

Body language—that is, the physical expression of interior blockage (or not, of course)—is an entire study in itself.

Dr. Anne Marie Bennstrom of the Ashram in Calabasas, California, has been studying what she calls "body types" for years. Since she is an expert physical culturist herself, she began to document the correlation between the language of the body and the blockages in consciousness of individuals whom she met and ultimately came to know. She says that in all her experience she never encountered a body that did not express, in physical terms, the internal attitudes of the consciousness it housed.

For example, a man with a short, squat body is predominantly interested in survival and in how his individual identity relates to home and hearth and material security. He is apt to be aggressive. Self-expression in a tall man, however, tends to appear as an overview tied to the future. "The short people are self-starters," says Bennstrom. "The tall men come in and take over to finish off the idea."

People with splayed, turned-out feet have energy that moves outward. They are outwardly motivated, always on the move, ready to travel, and often don't stop to think about what they are leaving behind. The splay-footed person throws caution to the winds and promises many things without thought of how to conserve the energy to accomplish any of them.

On the other hand (so to speak), pigeon-toed people tend to withhold their energy, sometimes tripping over their own best intentions. Such people tend also to be stubborn, defensive, and inflexible.

Anne Marie believes that the point of making these correlations is that changing the body attitude can assist in changing the emotional attitude. In working with people, if she reminds a pigeon-toed person to consciously turn the feet out more, the act itself affects the inner consciousness to be more outgoing.

The purpose, then, of altering the habits of a body type is to help an individual find "the middle way" and achieve more balance in life, to become more centered. If one can establish where the blockages lie, it is easier to offer advice on where that person should look for his own weakness.

The more balance we hold between the masculine and feminine (or yang and yin) in ourselves, the more streamlined our bodies become, because our bodies reflect our consciousness. Fat in any area equals emotion unexpressed. The more androgynously balanced we become, the less fat we hold. I do not mean androgynous in the sense of bisexuality, but androgynous as it relates to feeling equally balanced with the male and female aspects in ourselves.

There is an obvious link between human physicality and human consciousness. When the consciousness is expanded to include recognition of the esoteric and spiritual nature of man, the physical body reflects that recognition. Since physicality follows consciousness, we would do well to go to the source of our physical problems rather than to treat symptoms, although treating symptoms can free us to focus on the source.

Despite the dominance of traditional methods of medicine, there is an ever-increasing interest in exploring the roots of consciousness as a guide to a solution for physical suffering. And the roots of consciousness speak directly through the seven chakras of which the physical body is an expression.

To me, what is most attractive about this holistic approach is that it recognizes and honors the balancing of man's energies by means which acknowledge that we are more than simply physical beings.

8

Meditating on the Chakras

*Love transforms all it touches—
for as we grow in its light
we learn to love and be loved.*

Meditating on the chakras is a multi-level exercise and a wonder-filled experience. It involves inner concentration (the first step in all meditation), plus visualization and, later, the use of sound.

It is so complex that the simplest approach I can think of is just to describe what I do in this form of meditation.

Since I choose to be aligned *before* I get out of bed and begin my day, I usually do my chakra work just after I wake up. In that alpha state of consciousness that is conducive to hearing whispered guidance and directives from within, I lie in bed and begin with the base chakra. I visualize it as red and spin the wheel that I "know" is there. (The direction of the spin is unimportant. Some people prefer to see a pulse.) Sometimes I "see" the red of the energy center. Sometimes I don't. Whether I do or not, I accept that it exists and so, proceeding with my own acceptance, I spin the red chakra until sometimes I can feel the crimson heat of acceleration in the center of the base of my spine.

Since the base chakra deals with issues of earth-plane grounding and understanding of the physical dimension, I then direct my conscious mind to coalesce the emotional issues involved in my life and blend the corresponding feelings with the red as I spin. Since the base chakra governs adrenal responses of flight or fight, I allow myself to use the spinning as a calming influence on whatever I find myself afraid of.

Blockage in the base chakra is an indication that one's feelings have been conditioned to self-shame, unworthiness, and lack of understanding of one's functions. Those feelings need to be cleared and balanced. Then, in that state of balance, I communicate to the Earth my trust that she will treat me in direct ratio to how I treat her. That is the grounding process.

Some days I don't think of Mother Earth and my purpose for living on her at all. Some days I just simply "see" red and have to relax my anger by meditating on the red of the base chakra. When I come into alignment with it, the anger dissipates. If I'm having a problem with my kidneys, I meditate longer and spin the chakra faster because the base chakra governs the kidneys. If I feel sluggish and lacking in energy, I picture the adrenal glands and spin red energy to them because I know that the base chakra externalizes as the adrenals. It is not necessary to know exactly where the adrenals are. It *is* necessary to know that on some level you know.

I am an extremely willful person, so when I balance my base chakra (the chakra that channels the energies of human will) with the higher, more esoteric chakras of Divine vibration, I am much easier to be around. In other words, I blend together the red of the base chakra with the violet of the crown chakra and I feel better. When I forget or haven't taken the time, I can feel the imbalance, and frankly so do those around me.

After the base chakra, I move up to the second chakra, which is orange and is located in the reproductive area. This chakra governs physical and emotional issues of creativity and sexuality. The second chakra is the center of our physical origin. From it flows our creative energy and our attitudes to sin and guilt. When meditating upon it, it helps to visualize washing away those negative attitudes with a brilliant orange light. On a subliminal level I am aware that the red of the root chakra is still spinning, but my focus is on the orange.

Meditation on this chakra originated thousands of years ago in the Hindu traditions when the human body was considered to be a temple for experiencing sensual spirituality. The partners did not imagine their relationships ending in death but rather that they were tied in a Divine communion throughout eternity, to be physically experienced again whenever the decision for physical re-embodiment was made. Therefore, immediate sexual gratification and lust were not perspectives from which people conducted their sexual activities, which, today, too often result in anger, hurt, and resentment.

This was during the tantric time periods in ancient India when, as the Sanskrit texts tell us, sex neither joined people together when it was present nor broke them apart when it was absent. The two lives were connected, instead, by a grander feeling of total merging and creativity. They believed that the male and female were complementary experiences of energy exchanges, and that the second chakra was not solely the center of sexuality but more the place of "creative dwelling and origin."

Meditating on the second chakra is a way of confronting one's fear of being uncreative, unproductive. When successfully accomplished, it can put one in touch with the fundamental understanding that the body is basically an aggregate of universal particles that the Higher Self has sculpted to experience a physical existence and truly fulfill its purpose for that lifetime. When that mission is completed, the particles disperse and become part of the Earth (on which the life was experienced), which in time disperses the particles back to the universe. In meditating on the second chakra it becomes more clear that the Higher Self is never dispersed but is indeed the composer of the particles *and* of the symphony of life. The composer and the composed become one for a time, yet it is possible to make a distinction between the two.

I like to use a juicy orange as an image when I visualize the spinning of the second chakra. It feels pleasant to spill the juiciness of the orange color through the reproductive system, as it equalizes and cleanses any feelings of conflict, confusion, or concern. Since the second chakra governs one's attitudes in intimate and creative relationships, the juicy orange meditation is very satisfying.

It might be well to mention here that we have all visualized and meditated whether we call it that or not. For example, if we have had the experience of sexual fantasy, we have visualized. If we have visualized the fantasy until it affects the body (orgasm), then we see the power of the mind to affect the body. That same kind of process of visualization can be used to help heal the body.

Even though the chakra centers are spinning in their own colors naturally, it helps to augment their natural spinning by visualizing them doing so. Also, it is not so necessary to "see" the colors you are spinning as it is to remember the "sense" of what the colors look like. You are remembering the vibration of the color in any case. So if I have difficulty in visualizing red, for instance, I augment the visualization with the memory of a bright red apple, or a crimson ruby, or whatever shade of red gives me the most pleasure. The image of whatever I select to remember is enough to inspire the reality of the color I wish to meditate upon. It all takes practice. But with that practice color visualization becomes easier.

It is important to balance the third, or solar plexus, chakra, particularly if there is an emotional upset going on in your life. This is the chakra that governs our attitudes toward personal power and sensitivity and ego. The largest obstacle to our growth and balance of the third chakra is *ego*. Ego is connected to the fear of losing something, or some part of oneself, or someone. Out of that fear springs the need to manipulate, bully, or in other ways control the people in one's life. When we become attuned to the third chakra, we like ourselves better, feel more self-confident and are therefore more capable of breaking the restrictive bonds of negative ego.

Relationships that cause emotional upset are always about personal power and ego in relation to our sensitivities. I find that when I visualize and meditate on the yellow of the solar plexus chakra and direct the color to permeate my midsection, I begin to relax and "allow" whatever will be to be. The calming effect takes on a sunny yellow quality, and the vibration of whatever emotional upset I might be feeling subsides. The fat that I'm holding in that area also begins to disappear because fat is anger withheld and blocked.

Nature provides each of us with healing tools if we can just trust that their holistic power works. Again, that power depends on the belief that we entrust to it. Colors are tools with power and are applicable to the extent that we wish to use them.

To bathe the pancreas, which governs the actions of the liver, spleen, stomach, and gallbladder, in yellow light, is to contribute to the calming and relaxation of the nervous system. How we abuse, misuse, or don't use our personal power is directly related to the balance of the third chakra. I find it fascinating that one of the deepest insults we can visit on someone is to call him or her "yellow," meaning cowardly; what it really means is that they are lacking in the personal enactment of their own power out of insecurity. When the third chakra is recognized by the conscious mind as healthily spinning in balance, and is reinforced as to the role it plays not only in your physical life but in your emotional life as well, the effect is startling.

Yellow is a sunny color. The sun is the source of our warmth and power. It makes us feel good. It lightens our spirits. We cannot be without its warm yellow light for very long. It is possible to create the feeling of a warm internal sun with the power of visualization so that the sensitivities we feel can be reassured by the acceptance of our own personal power, which is the governing province of the solar plexus chakra. When that occurs, the stomach, liver, gallbladder, and spleen are relaxed and vibrating at a more even frequency and our problems of egotism are reduced.

By bringing in some orange, we merge the creative

and sexual energies of the second chakra into the sensitivities and personal power of the third chakra. If we mix red along with this balance we are grounding our understanding of the emotional balance achieved into our physical relationship with the Earth, which contributes to ridding ourselves of fear and other fight-or-flight conflicts of the first chakra.

So the panoply of emotional and physical issues that we express through the seven chakras can be modified, balanced, and aligned by consciously playing with the color vibrations of the rainbow, using our body as an instrument. Colors are at our disposal every moment of our lives and are in fact operating and spinning in harmony whether we consciously recognize them or not.

Once again, we are what we are consciously aware of. To be more aware of the value of our chakra system is to be more aware of our internal power. And to be aware of internal power is to understand the potential for external power. We can create whatever we want on the exterior by recognizing what power is hidden on the interior. The game of life then becomes *how* we create that power externally and what we do with it when it is ours: which brings us to an examination of the four chakras above the solar plexus.

Since the fourth chakra governs the heart, when we meditate and visualize the green of it, we are in effect stimulating it to be more effective in governing the love feelings that also harmonize the immune and endocrine systems. The radiation produced by love flow can heal the entire body.

Meditating on the heart chakra will help the process of learning to love oneself so that the love of others is more possible. The self-confidence derived from it will carry a subtle vibration that will be felt by family, friends, and co-workers. We receive from others what we have already seen and created in ourselves. An inner security will create security in others. All of that centers in the heart.

Sometimes when I meditate, I begin with the heart chakra because everything in our lives essentially flows from the heart. I visualize the green as brilliant emerald and I remember that the Earth is called the green planet. The vibration of green is soothing and generates life. On Earth, there is more green than any other color because the planet is vibrating with life.

Sometimes when I am working with my chakra meditations I infuse the green of the heart chakra into the yellow of the solar plexus before I move the mixture down to the orange and red chakras. There are so many ways to play with this kind of color therapy that it becomes an adventure within the theater of my own consciousness. Soon I begin to feel the differences in color vibrational frequency, and I operate accordingly.

For example, the colors I choose to wear during the day have a decided effect on my consciousness. To wear bright green is a definitive statement because of the frequency attached. People speak of being green with jealousy because they feel deprived of attention and love.

When we are red with anger or fear, we are feeling the symptoms of the fight-or-flight first-chakra syndrome. To wear red when feeling anger only reinforces the feeling unless mixed with another color. To counteract it with heart green helps quell the rage with the vibration of the heart.

The fifth chakra, known as the throat chakra, is one all of us would do well to recognize and meditate upon. Since it is the center through which we communicate and express ourselves, it is also the center through which we formulate judgments of others. It also governs the organs that translate air into expression: lungs, vocal cords, and the bronchial tubes.

Since this is the chakra of judgment and expression, when meditating it helps to literally let go of any ill feelings we are harboring toward anyone. I usually begin by asking myself why I feel resentment. Is it crushed expectations? Bitterness born out of rejection? Do I feel cheated in some way? Whatever. In so many ways we feel alienated from people because of a buildup of anger in our own minds. Thus, we become bonded to those people through anger, which serves only to perpetuate the ill feeling.

To let go sounds simple, and actually it is simple— but it is not an easy thing to do. We cling to hate, or anger, as to an anchor. And indeed, feelings do anchor us. Anger gives us a dramatic role, fires us up, creates energy, defines a relationship. It even anchors us with the unconscious fear of what will fill the gap if we get rid of it! But when we *are* able to let anger go, relief floods in, love flows in. When we see that love is the glue that holds everything together, we realize it is the channel of communication between souls, not just between people. The same judgments we made that were rejected by others will now be understood and welcomed because the new energy behind them is positive. In fact, we will know better when to speak, when not to, and how to do it with more influence because we are anchored in love.

Whenever I'm feeling that I'm not understood, I meditate with blue on the throat chakra in order to clear out the blockages which prevent me from being clear. If it's a sexual misunderstanding, I mix orange with it. If it's an emotional problem with my own personal power, I mix yellow with the blue. And if I want to be especially loving in the way I tell someone the harsh truth, I mix heart green with the blue.

Blockage in the throat chakra can also be caused by fear of speaking your own truth. To constantly attempt to please others while sacrificing your own true expression can develop into a deep frustration of communication.

Every time I am about to say something harsh about someone, I try to remember to visualize blue mixed with a beautiful heart green before I speak.

That way, I not only spare them my harshness, but I spare myself the karmic inevitability of my harshness returning to me. Of course, most of the time I am so caught up in my own judgment and the need to express it that I forget. Much of this can be alleviated by the discipline of meditating on each of the colors the chakras represent as a path to the feelings you want to explore. Soon your awareness expands to such an extent that in applying it to your life, you find your experience of living has improved. It has improved because you are consciously acknowledging alignment.

To me, the miracle of all of it is that the alignment is always there whether we are aware of it or not; but only through conscious acknowledgment, only through deliberate recognition of our natural harmony, do we derive its strength. We are what we're conscious of.

The sixth chakra is the third eye or face chakra. It is located behind the center of the forehead, a very visible area. It is the chakra that governs the way we present ourselves to the world. If our faces are pinched with worry and anxiety, they can be relaxed by meditating on the color indigo, which allows us to resonate to our inner vision, our idealism, and our imagination. Since the third eye chakra externalizes as the pituitary gland, it governs much of our lower brain and nervous system. This chakra also controls all of our incoming and outgoing thoughts and visions. It is the center of the eye of awareness.

The energy from within can be used any way we

wish. Our *choice* of thoughts is what determines its external manifestation. Through our third eye we can harness and orchestrate our God-given energy within.

I use the third eye (sixth chakra) meditation whenever I want to manifest an outer vision for myself. The tapestry potential of painting our lives with color and feeling is unlimited, and the more I work with the spiritual metaphysical elements of vibrational energy, the more I accomplish and the more fun it is.

The seventh chakra has the highest vibrational frequency of all. The color violet oscillates faster than any other single color, which stands to reason because the crown chakra is the center for final Divine integration. The higher we go, the more clearly can we see where we come from. This is true physically and spiritually.

Seen from the crown chakra, anger gives way to understanding, hate gives way to love, possessiveness gives way to freedom.

From this vantage point it is easier to see how dark emotions of fear, depression, hatred, and so on sap our energy, which ultimately results in illness.

Problems that have loomed gigantic now seem silly, not because they are smaller but because we are bigger than they are.

Seeing our existence in this new light makes possibilities limitless. *And* it develops a sense of compassion for others who don't see it yet. You see yourself in them and you remember how difficult it was.

People's actions are always determined by the way they see themselves in the world.

It is said that when someone experiences the violet flame, he or she is resonating in total alignment with the God force within.

Whenever we feel the need to spiritualize any of the "lower" chakras and corresponding emotions, we need to integrate the color violet as we visualize and meditate while at the same time infusing the awareness of the Divine frequency that it represents. It is important to focus not only on the colors associated with the chakras but to integrate those colors with the connected emotions you are trying to resolve. Ultimately the language of color can heal. Thus, healing is basically a successful alignment of the conscious mind with the spiritual centers.

When my chakras are aligned and cleansed, I usually combine all the light frequencies of each color together, and above my head I visualize a bright and brilliant white light. White light is the combination of all light frequencies.

The white light that many people describe during out-of-body experiences could be said to represent the infusion of all emotional frequencies, which, when perfectly realized, become the essence of God.

Therefore, when you surround yourself with a bubble of white light, you are in essence surrounding yourself with the light of God, in the center of which you are always protected, loved, and in turn loving.

Once again you become that which you visualize God to be.

It might seem implausible or irrelevant to discuss visualization and meditative techniques in a world that appears so hopelessly lacking in spiritual recognition, but it is for just this reason that such techniques for spiritual discipline become more and more necessary. Without the acknowledgment and conscious awareness of our sadly unrecognized spiritual technology, we will, it seems to me, become more and more isolated from our purpose in being alive. To be separated from the knowledge of one's destiny and purpose is truly a disaster.

More and more people are awakening to this. More and more people are scientifically, socially, politically, and economically seeing themselves not only as physical and intellectual beings but spiritual beings as well. Maybe even *fundamentally* spiritual beings.

We are in an age of enlightenment now, which means "to be in knowledge of." We are becoming more "in knowledge" of ourselves. It doesn't matter if a person is a Christian, Moslem, Hindu, Jew, or an atheist. There is a wealth of knowledge to be tapped. The individual has his own relationship to the God within, irrespective of the church he belongs to. The power within is an untapped power available to all of us who seek it for whatever use we want or need to make of it. None of our institutions are addressing themselves to that truth. Each individual has the right and the duty to use the potential knowledge of harmony and alignment within. We are at a cross-roads of integrating the physical and the spiritual, with the role of consciousness just beginning to be understood.

It is time for spiritual technology to become specifically understood and taught. Use of meditation upon the chakras allows a person to envisage the world that lies within and to benefit from it. Opening our inner pathways permits access to power but it is a power available only through love.

Love is obviously a word used—and abused—by most of us. Within the circles where a spiritual search is taking place, it is a word evoked more often than any other. The need for ways to freely give and receive love is basically what motivates spiritual curiosity. I believe this need is what we all long to fulfill.

I had a close friend who was dying of AIDS. He was making his adjustments to what was happening to him, going through various stages of denial and acceptance of his fate.

On Good Friday of 1988 he called me with a question: "How do you accept love from others?" he asked. "Do you find it painful? Can you let it in?"

I didn't know how to answer. I had never really thought about love based on the certainty of being bereft of all those I had to leave behind by dying.

Did one want to, as it were, shut off? Under such circumstances, what did love mean? I tried to think of some comparable situation that might hold some answers for my friend.

I remembered my father as he lay dying. He seemed so peaceful, so ready to go. He couldn't move his arms or legs but he could talk a little, very slowly. I'll never forget how he looked into my eyes and said, "Nothing matters but love . . . nothing in this world . . . not possessions, not fame, not even what you do. Only love."

He didn't say any more. But with those words and the look in his eyes I understood something grand, something even more than any of my spiritual studying had taught me.

And now someone else close to me was grappling with the same question. But his attitude was entirely different from that of my father. I could not really find anything to say except, "Yes, always accept love."

Good Friday passed and so did the next day. On Easter morning I woke, alone in my house in the Pacific Northwest. The sky was cloudy. Raindrops glistened on the high trees outside my window. A streak of sun shone through suddenly.

I asked myself, "What does Easter really mean?"

I got up and went outside. The sun had disappeared and rain began to fall; first a misty drizzle, then a downpour.

I decided to go swimming in the rain. In the water I thought about love. What would it feel like to love completely, wholly, over a lifetime, first with the driving, urgent, agonized need of youth, then the exchange of maturity, rich and full of fun and strength, and finally with the sweet, enduring love of age: I thought about all the other kinds of love there are, the unquestioning, totally giving nature of a beloved pet, the joyful innocence of loving one's children, the happy, affectionate respect between friends, often accompanied by real devotion—my God, the world was full of love. I don't know how much time elapsed. The raindrops fell on my head like chilled beads. It occurred to me that it was possible to love each and every one of those raindrops into warmth. I tried to isolate each of them and as they landed I savored and appreciated and loved each with a warm welcome. Soon I realized that I wasn't aware of chill. I had shifted a cold experience by perceiving it to be warm.

It came as a mini-revelation. I climbed out of the swimming pool and stood up expecting to feel more rain on my body. Instead, as if on cue from some master lighting designer in the sky, the sun came out and the rain stopped. It was so immediate, so much like stepping onstage into the "spot," that I felt myself smiling all over.

I headed for the house, thinking no more about it: got dressed and prepared to take my dogs for a walk down the mountain to the river. The sun was shining, and it would be a beautiful Easter hike.

I walked outside, the dogs leaping and gamboling beside me, and as I took the first step down the mountain path, not only did the sun disappear, but a rain cloud opened above us and spilled everything in it! I hadn't even seen a cloud a moment before. It was a different kind of welcome, but I couldn't help laughing. I called to Sultan and Shinook and went back inside. As soon as I closed the door, the sun came out again.

I was intrigued. I immediately took the dogs out again. And immediately, as if on cue, the sun disappeared and the rain came down again. Was nature playing hide-and-seek with me, or was it a coincidence?

We ran back inside. The sun came out. We went outside, the rain started. Back and forth, back and forth. It was beginning to look like a vaudeville act. The dogs were very confused. But they didn't give up, gamely following me in and out, all of us growing breathless.

Finally we went out again. But first I stood at the top of the mountain path and said out loud, "You're playing games with me, aren't you? Especially for Easter!" I didn't know who I was talking to and it was all so ridiculous that I started to laugh again. The sun blazed! It was as though nature (God . . . whatever) needed acknowledgment of its power and, having secured it, no longer needed to play tricks.

Together the three of us set out again to trek down the mountain. A gentle breeze drifted over us. The dogs bounded ahead of me and I returned to my thoughts about love, about Easter, about nature.

Could one start to feel *complete* love by beginning with nature?

I walked by the river for an hour, then started back up the mountain. The sun, like an orange balloon, played tag with the clouds, chasing them away whenever they came too close.

As I trudged up the steep mountain path I was aware of how easily the dogs scaled the heights on their four feet and sensibly organized forms. There seemed to be no pain for them, their powerful bodies responding with natural ease to the terrain. But my legs hurt, my heart pounded, and in general I was again reminded of how lazy I could really be because I basically hated physical exercise that caused me pain. Then, in light of the morning's experience, something occurred to me. Why not try loving the pain? Why not completely appreciate the experience with every muscle and sinew? *Feel* what each was doing, concentrate on the miracle of coordination that was my body? I began to alter my perception of the difficulties of the climb. I told myself that with each movement I was more conscious of what made up my body and that without the love of that awareness I wouldn't even know I had a body. I caressed the pain, I felt it *work*, I welcomed it. I specifically isolated each muscle and tendon and loved the feel of them just as I had loved the feel of each chilled raindrop on my head.

Pretty soon I realized I had forgotten I was climbing; in fact, I was moving strongly, light and easy with the terrain. The shift in reality that accompanied the shift in my perspective was really remarkable.

In the midst of this experience I thought of my friend with AIDS. His body lay inert, with no energy. Its demeaning and foul symptoms battered his spirit. He was angry with himself for allowing this—indeed for creating it. And angry at his doctors for not being able to heal him. Should I tell him about what I had just done? Could I have the temerity to ask him to give up his anger? To try to heal himself through self-love? Would it be outrageously insulting to suggest that taking responsibility for his horrible disease might be the beginning of a healing process, that it might be possible to understand and even to love his decision? Could I really say that fighting with hate was not the answer, that relaxing into love of wholeness might give him a much better chance and that to accept the love of others could be a literal tonic? I knew that at the very least, persuading him to accept the horrors for what they were would make them a whole lot easier to bear. That was something love could do.

I reached the top of the mountain. The sun still shone brilliantly. I stood for a moment, breathing in the crisp sun-drenched breeze, thinking, "God, I'm lucky." And then, "Love must be what Easter is all about." I opened my arms and said, "Thank you. I think I've just understood something about the power of healing that feeling love can accomplish."

As if in answer, and as suddenly as anything I've

ever experienced, I found myself standing in the center of a crystal hailstorm showering down while beyond the sun continued to shine. Thousands of balls of shimmering ice diamonds sparkled and danced and glistened like a shining curtain that gently enveloped me. I was in a fairyland that spoke to me of natural miracles if I would only open up and listen. I stretched my arms out to catch the falling diamonds, feeling their icy burn in the palms of my hands. I looked up. There above me, through the airborne curtain and on the other side of it, I watched a circular rainbow form.

There they were, the seven colors coming into pristine clarity. Those were the same seven colors reflected inside me. I stood still, awestruck for a moment, drinking in the exquisite display. One by one, beginning with the red on the lower part of the rainbow, I watched each color until the violet appeared at the top.

Nature had spoken. I allowed the message to touch me. At first I thought I would cry. But I found myself smiling, glowing inside. I went right in and called my friend. We talked about chakras and he began to meditate and work with those natural, harmonious, unrecognized energy centers of his body.

He stayed alive nearly half a year longer than his doctors had expected. Before he finally reached the end he told me and other close friends that the great lesson he had learned from his disease was that of allowing himself to accept love. He had never had a problem giving love. His was the problem of allowing himself to believe that others really loved him. Because he had been reluctant to nourish himself with the love of others his body had reflected that bereavement.

One evening, on the night of his last birthday, his closest friends gathered in his living room to say goodbye. We watched him walk in, proud and elegant in his satin robe and silk pyjamas. He sat quietly in the midst of the group while, one by one, we expressed our love for him. He accepted our offering with an open heart, and with an acceptance of his fate. He was, at last, at peace with himself.

After he passed on, those of us who had been with him that evening realized we had formed the nucleus of a new family, a family that revolved around the understanding that our friend, whom we would miss so much, had been one of our greatest teachers. His profound lesson? Learn to love self and accept love from others. Don't wait until you are deathly sick to feel you deserve love.

9

Crystals

Our palate for the taste of life has become numb
because we have forgotten how to dream.

The first time someone gave me a natural quartz crystal I laid it in the palm of my hand to examine it. I was fascinated. Not only was it beautiful: it seemed to have dimensions within dimensions, reflections within reflections. I held it up to the sun and allowed myself to sort of go inside it. It had six sides and the sunlight made it act as a prism, refracting the seven colors of the rainbow.

It had meant so much to the person who gave it to me. I held it in my hand, feeling uninformed and inadequate about what I was holding. What was the significance, beyond its beauty, of this mineral that seemed to speak to so many? I realized that lots of people were giving one another crystals. There were crystals of every color and configuration. What did it all mean? I began to read books on crystals. I found I was meeting people who called themselves "crystal workers." Their expertise seemed vast and detailed.

This is some of what I learned.

The Earth is a living, breathing, evolving entity, just as we are. It has force fields of subtle energies, just as we do. It has veins and arteries of minerals and substances that carry with them storehouses of energy that receive and transmit constantly. Crystals, I learned, were mineral transmitters and receivers of cosmic energy buried in the Earth. As I read and learned about crystals I realized that wherever ground was considered sacred and holy there were large crystal deposits buried underneath. In folklore and among Indian tribes it was believed that crystals provided a path to amplification of life force from the Great Spirit. Mountain people claimed crystals relayed cosmic secrets to man, that they held thought forms and important mysteries from the past. . . . I learned, listened, and wondered. I knew that crystals amplify sound waves in a radio receiver, or light waves in a television receiver. Could they also amplify thought waves of consciousness in the human brain receiver? Were they, in effect, living expressions of cosmic consciousness?

When I was in Egypt I learned that during the time of the pharaohs the ancient function of crystal gemstones was to heal and to provide amplification of each appropriately colored chakra center while meditating upon it. The value of these gems increased through the ages. They seemed to be precious not only because they were rare but because they were needed as healing tools. The ruby, I learned, was used to heal problems governed by the red, base chakra. Topaz and carnelian were used to heal problems governed by the orange, sexual chakra. Yellow sapphire and citrine were used for the solar plexus. Emerald for the heart. Blue sapphire for the throat. Lapis lazuli for the third eye. And amethyst for the crown chakra. White diamonds, which include the light of all colors, became the gem that usually surrounded the others for even further amplification. The greed for gemstones, then, seemed to be originally based upon the desire for amplified health and balance. The nature of crystals and gemstones had a more intimate connection with our lives than I had thought.

Quartz crystal was thought of as the master gemstone. In its functions of healing, quartz crystal had properties that interlinked with at least three of the seven main chakras: the third, solar plexus chakra; the fifth, heart chakra; and the sixth, third eye or face chakra. With crystal amplification these chakras could interlink more effectively with the crown chakra.

I felt as though I was unraveling the real reasons why so many human beings were fascinated by and driven to possess jewels. They seemed to be unconsciously understanding that these many-faceted gems were a gateway to increased consciousness, possibly tools for health, the light to understanding self. Crystals seemed to have properties that were useful in projecting thought forms and storing thought forms dealing with broad universal consciousness.

In nearly all cultures they had been used for centuries as healing tools. They had been used as a point of focus in meditation and had been one of the primary substances in confirming the vibration and concept of invisible or ethereal energy.

I learned that the use of quartz crystals and gemstones went all the way back to the ancient civilizations of India and beyond, even to Lemuria (a continent that is said to have existed where the Pacific Ocean is now). Then they were regarded as cornerstones for the process of thought amplification, whereby, with applied electromagnetic voltage, one's brain waves could be broadcast through the ethers. Red crystals contained fire energy. Blue crystals, water energy. Clear crystals, air energy. Crystals with two colors represented a balancing of energies.

Quartz crystals were also planted alongside seeds and when meditated upon would significantly increase the speed and size of the seeds' growth. Crystals, said the books, had their own rates of vibration, just as everything does. A slow-vibrating crystal was a wonderful tool for deep meditation. Crystals with a faster vibrating spectrum helped people to relate to higher levels of cosmic consciousness.

Quartz crystals were used to increase the effectiveness of many other therapies. For example, if acupuncture points were stimulated by stainless steel needles with part of the shaft coated with quartz crystal, there was an enhancement of the therapy's effectiveness. This is because the life force stimulated by the manipulation of the needles would help dispel the negative energy blocking that point.

To attune to the seven chakras more quickly, people would lie down and place a quartz crystal on each chakra desired and tune in to the corresponding color and vibrational frequency. The crystal accelerated the amplification of the consciousness to each chakra.

I became so fascinated with what I learned that I began to experiment with crystals myself. In a darkened room I placed the crystal given to me at eye level on a high table. Then I lit a candle behind it and sat down next to it. I gazed into the crystal and projected positive and loving thought forms into it. I had the feeling that they reverberated back to me. It was very pleasant. Then I tried negative and angry thought forms. I had the feeling that that is what I got back. I became uncomfortable. I made my choice. For an hour I sat in front of my crystal with the candle behind it and just gazed into it with thoughts that were as pleasant as I could conjure up. It was a wonderful evening. And I slept better than I had in weeks. Maybe the crystal was a powerful tool in amplifying the positive thought waves in my mind just as they amplified sound waves in a radio or light waves in a TV.

Another time I asked a friend of mine to try an experiment with me. We sat facing each other in a darkened room with several quartz crystals at eye level between us on a glass table. Again I lit a candle.

This time *below* the crystal. Then I put on some soft music and when we stopped giggling we gazed into each other's eyes through the illuminated crystals. We attuned to our seven chakras while doing this (he was on his own spiritual search!) and soon we each felt a deeper attunement to the other on an esoteric and spiritual level. Slowly we found we were feeling a more profound understanding of each other's sensitivities. It was wonderful, particularly when we allowed ourselves to take it seriously. It sort of cemented our friendship, and we have exchanged crystals ever since.

A few couples I know apply this technique. They say they feel they are working directly to harmonize the flow of their chakras and all the emotions that these entail. They say this technique brings them into a truer understanding of the inner nature of each other. Disruptive attitudes disappear. False values fall away, and the emotional sharing that develops as a result of the spiritual honesty allows them to confront difficult issues that might otherwise take them years to have the courage to explore. When these issues are confronted and shared, a cleansing occurs and deeper harmony results.

Now, whenever I am feeling out of sorts, I balance my chakra system with the use of whatever crystal is my favorite at the time. Let me say here that crystals almost speak to individual human beings. They seem to say "I belong to you." However, very soon one realizes that crystals are not to be owned permanently. They are to be enjoyed and passed on.

It is necessary to cleanse your crystals about once a month to rid them of a buildup of negative energy. (Crystals store negative as well as positive energy.)

The process of cleansing is very simple. Immerse the crystal in salt water (preferably sea salt instead of table salt) and apple cider vinegar and leave it out in the sunlight for about a day.

When working with any healing stone you are well advised to cleanse it even if no one else has handled it.

I have been told that another good use of crystals is to put one on top of your TV. It draws in the radiation that color TV emits. Remove it every three months and cleanse it in sea salt for a day to draw out the radiation. Be careful to pick up the crystal from the TV with a cloth; otherwise, you are absorbing radiation from the TV into your body.

When I meditate for healing purposes, I place a colored stone (gem quality is not necessary, the color is all that matters) on the chakra that requires the most attention. (A small piece of surgical tape will keep it in place.) Then I "breathe" in the color of the stone to the chakra that I feel is blocked.

If I'm emotionally upset over something, I know my solar plexus chakra can use some help: yellow stone. If I'm afraid, my base chakra needs attention: red stone. If I feel a lack of creativity, I use an orange stone and breathe in orange to my second chakra, et cetera. . . . This is what is meant by holistic healing, or at least it is one of the methods.

Some people prefer to swallow gemstone elixirs, which are derived by placing a stone in clear water for a day in the sunlight. The vibration of the stone is conducted by the water.

However one wishes to use quartz crystals and gemstones, it would be well to realize that the real healing comes with the enhancement of meditation and creative visualization. Don't rely on the crystals and gemstones to do it for you. The consciousness brought to the exercise is *everything*.

The process of aligning the mind, body, and spirit through meditation and visualization with the aid of a crystal makes you an active healer of your own malady. By calming and stilling the mind and by allowing the integration and intervention of the spirit, you become a more fully realized human being, recognizing that you are functioning on a spiritual as well as mind and body levels. Therefore, through the activation of your conscious awareness, you are affecting your body.

With the increase in spiritual awareness, the human being unifies and raises the body frequency, which in turn manufactures an increase in energy flow.

So, meditation with color visualization, meditation with colored stones placed on the chakra centers, and the ingestion of colored-gem elixirs are pleasant and subtle ways of self-healing and aligning the mind, body, and spirit.

But the most immediate and convenient technique

in a crisis is "color breathing." For example, if you need to understand the reason you have created the dinner to burn just before guests arrive, try turning off the stove and relax for a moment. Breathe in violet or indigo air. Simply picture the air as violet. Let the color live in its vividness in your mind's eye, relax again, and breathe it in. Not only can breathing violet be calming, but because it is the color of Divine purpose, you might find the cosmic lesson in the burned meat!

I keep a necklace of colored stones with me at all times. If I need to remind myself of the blue of sapphire before I breathe in blue, I lift the colored stone to the sun (a small stone is fine), register the blue in my memory, and immediately translate the blue of the stone to the air I'm breathing.

Breathing pink is extremely calming. Pink is the color of human Divinity. Some prisons—for instance, Attica and Folsom—are now using pink on the walls of rooms that house particularly disturbed criminals. There are those in spiritually advanced circles who claim that a new energy center is developing in the human being located between the throat and the heart. It is being referred to as the "peace" chakra and its color is pink.

Color breathing is as much fun as it is healing. And it is amusing and tender for me to realize that the tools for health and alignment are all at our disposal simply by allowing our consciousness to become aware and to access them. And they are free.

✦

The day after the Cleveland seminar I traveled to Canada to visit the famous Crystal Skull, owned and cared for by the woman who found it in an archaeological dig in South America with her father, Sir Michael Mitchel-Hedges, seventy years before. It is clearly one of the wonders of the world, a museum piece extraordinaire, but Anna promised her father and the natives from whose land it was excavated that she would always personally care for it. All involved understood that the Crystal Skull needed contact and human attention.

I walked into Anna's living room and saw it there on her coffee table. She gestured for me to pick it up and hold it. I did. It was heavy, about twelve pounds. As soon as I held it I felt as though it responded to me. It was so pleasantly strange. I sat on the floor with the skull in my lap; then, for some reason, rolled it around on the carpet. I could have sworn I felt it laugh with enjoyment. It seemed alive. Anna said everyone who had held it had similar reactions. She smiled at me and very quietly left the room.

I lay on the floor and held the skull up to the light. I thought I saw dimensions and other worlds swim in and out of my mind's eye as the connection with the crystal amplified my thoughts. (Mitchel-Hedges believed the crystal was an Atlantean relic that has communicated its identity down through the ages.) Finally I lay down and placed the skull on my chest and meditated. Again I felt it communicate to me. Pictures from other times and other places swam in front of my eyes. It was as though I needed to see them, and somehow on a visceral level I knew I was looking at parts of my past and clearing away emotional debris. I fell into a kind of sleep-reverie and experienced myself in an Atlantean temple of some kind. The walls were crystal and the human beings who sat meditating were androgynous-looking. A perfect balance of male and female. Suddenly there was my father, dressed in a crystal-fabric robe, giving a lecture. He wasn't speaking, though. He was teaching through thought transference! The lesson was on the importance of balancing the yin-female and the yang-male in every human being. Then he instructed everyone to concentrate on the second chakra, the sexual center. Just as he emphasized the *second* chakra, Anna's grandfather clock struck two. I came out of the meditation. I had been meditating for two hours! Such alternative realities there are to experience when one allows oneself the adventure.

10

Sound Meditation

———————— ❖ ————————

Listen to the sounds beyond silence.

Sound is an infinitely important part of my life. Harsh noise drives me crazy. Loud voices seem immature and temperamentally disturbed to me. Traffic noise seems unnatural because it drowns out the sounds of nature. I have never been able to adjust to the technological sound pollutants that progress has created. A peaceful, natural silence is heaven for me, and when I go through long periods deprived of that natural silence it affects my well-being. Consequently, meditating with sounds that heal became important to me.

Man's scientific instruments and his five senses can detect so-called solids because they are obviously physical. Solids are also characterized by their very slow vibrations.

Then comes sound, which ranges from 16 to 32,768 vibrations per second.

Steven Halpern, in his book *Sound Health,* proposes that vibrations at 1,000 cycles per second are easily audible. If you double the vibrations to 2,000 cycles per second, that equals one octave higher. If, on a piano keyboard, we could extend its range another fifty octaves higher, the keys, when struck at the higher end, would produce colors rather than audible sounds. Color vibrates at 500 billion cycles per second.

The color of light is expressed in various vibrations depending on the individual color. If we could "hear" colors in a musical language, the harmonics would be about forty octaves higher than audible sound.

There are seven notes on a Western scale of music. (The eighth note sounds the same as the first, but is eight notes higher—that is what makes it an octave.) There are seven colors in the rainbow. There are seven energy centers in the body. There are seven colors that correspond to those seven energy centers, and the mystics say there are seven levels of consciousness: physical, etheric, emotional, mental, astral, spiritual, and soul.

Each color of the chakra system resonates to its corresponding level of consciousness as well as to its note on the scale. In other words, if the vibration of the color red (first, base chakra) could be heard, it would resonate to the keynote of C on the scale. The color of the second chakra, orange, would resonate to the keynote of D. And so it goes up the scale. Each color has a corresponding note. Therefore, when meditating on a chakra color, augment the meditation by humming the note that each color corresponds to.

Red	=	C
Orange	=	D
Yellow	=	E
Green	=	F
Blue	=	G
Indigo	=	A
Violet	=	B

I found that meditating with color and sound on each of my chakra centers was helpful in making me feel more harmonious.

Sometimes I meditate and chant the sound "Om" with each chakra color. It was difficult at first to combine the two, but with practice it not only became easier but actually felt natural.

Om is said to be the original audible word best duplicating the vibration of God. It is a "power" word and has been used for centuries to instill harmony in healing. Actually, Om is an easy, soothing sound to hum, coming from deep in the throat and chest. When I chant it over and over it puts me in touch with the center of my being. I found that the longer I chanted Om, the deeper the state of my consciousness became.

However, since I didn't want to become a monk, I stopped chanting Om for *deep* meditative purposes. I use it now for color and sound alignment of the chakras. I let the sound reverberate in the center of myself until I feel it touch the place where I feel my soul connect with the universe. The energy I feel is soothing and therapeutic.

I first learned how effective sound could be *internally* when I began singing lessons. I couldn't understand why I felt so much more centered after a lesson. And it really didn't matter what my voice sounded like—it was the effect of the vibration on my solar plexus, heart, and so on. I remembered how diathermy, which is the therapy of sound waves, was a favorite with dancers and athletes whenever an injury was sustained.

Since I am so sensitive to sound, I travel with a white-sound machine that duplicates the gentle sound of ocean waves. (Actually it has rain, waterfall, *Surf I*, and *Surf II*!) Whenever I am in cities, particularly to sleep through traffic noise, I use the white-sound waves (*Surf II*) to drown out the sound pollution from below.

I think we are all sensitive to sounds in ways that are not measurable. Harsh sounds can affect our minds and bodies and spirits in very deleterious ways. Conversely, beautiful music and the peaceful, rhythmic sounds of nature nourish us. We are like receiver sets attuned to incoming and outgoing electromagnetic vibrations. We have highly attuned nervous systems, which, when violated, can make us sick and anxious.

The Schumann resonance is an equation which

concludes that the human system vibrates at a basic rate of about 7.8 to 8 cycles per second, which is inaudible when it is relaxed. The frequency of brain waves produced in meditation is also in the 8-cycles-per-second range.

Physicists claim that the Earth itself vibrates at 8 cycles per second. The nervous systems of all life forms are attuned to this basic frequency. Thus, there is an invisible harmonic resonance between the Earth, as a living vibrating entity, and the human being when in a relaxed state. When we humans are hyper or tense we are out of balance with the resonating frequencies of the Earth itself. Feeling in harmony with ourselves and the Earth then becomes a natural marriage of electromagnetic vibrations.

When we listen to beautiful music, the oscillation of the music vibration usually massages the tissues and cells, which in turn effect a balance that improves blood circulation, metabolism, and the pulsation of the endocrine glands. Music may be the universal language because it helps each of us to vibrate as one. For instance, the earliest forms of music—the tapping together of sticks, hand clapping, tapping on stretched skins, repetitive grunts and hums—were devices to express rhythmic sound, which is vibration.

Along those lines, I was interested in what Steven Halpern had to say about the phenomenon of what is called *Entrainment*. That is to say, whenever two or more oscillators in the same energy field are vibrating at almost the same rhythm, they tend to shift their respective rhythms until they are vibrating at *exactly* the same level. That is cosmic law—natural law. Entrainment is happening not only within our own individual bodies but is occurring with one another. We will shift to one another until we find a common rhythm. Therefore, if there is *anyone* suffering, we will all not only feel it but adjust our own rhythm to include it. Hence, one individual is everyone else's concern.

When we are each in tune with ourselves, we significantly affect the attunement of others. When we are seriously out of "sync" with ourselves, we also disrupt, disturb, and distress others. This is why someone who is aggressively skeptical *can* affect or even distort the effectiveness of "sensitives."

So, using color meditation and sound therapy helped me feel more peaceful, which in turn made me feel more healthy. I think more people could learn to use these techniques and to take responsibility for their own attunement as the first step toward recognizing that they have the right to experience themselves as harmonious.

According to science, the universe is an extremely harmonious place. Everything moves toward alignment and order. We humans, through our own self-judgment, actually seem to feel more comfortable with distortion and discord. But I think that is beginning to change as we see that happiness is a *choice* we make. Happiness requires attunement, and at-

tunement requires knowledge, and knowledge requires discipline in order to apply it. Holistic and
self-healing knowledge is a gift we have not yet
allowed ourselves to accept. We still put our trust
predominantly in medical authority, which by its
very definition treats disease rather than encouraging
the individual to stimulate his or her own self-healing
process. But even in this area, some physicians are
beginning to admit the power of individual belief as
an aid to recovery.

We are not simply a collection of chemicals that
can be treated with drugs. We are electromagnetic
beings and we can help ourselves in many ways. Man
has responses to the vibrations he is aware of, such
as sound, electricity, heat, light, and color. Beyond
this range, though, there is a vibrational field of
reality that human senses cannot yet perceive, but
which our scientific instruments can detect. The X
ray, for example, oscillates at 2 trillion vibrations per
second.

There is a vibrational continuum in nature, but
even science can detect only a limited level of that
continuum.

Beyond all these realities lie higher planes of reality with even faster vibrations, about which Western
science still knows little. These include the etheric
realms, the astral, the mental, and the spiritual planes.
And each plane of existence and reality obeys its own
laws and principles.

Since each human being is Divine in essence and

carries the vibration of the Divine within, he or she can be healed of many ills by touching and visualizing and meditating on the higher velocities of spiritual vibration. This is the basis of individuals said to have "healing hands." The body is a byproduct of the mind and spirit. Energy follows thought. Body follows consciousness. In fact, our physical world depends on what we consciously project and perceive it to be.

So the process of working with visualizations coupled with sound or music, allowing the harmonics of the notes to soothe and quell tension and stress, is available to anyone who is prepared to take the responsibility of trusting the internal harmony to merge with exterior vibration.

Here's one of the processes I use:

I draw a hot bath at a time when I know I won't be disturbed. I turn off the telephone. I place my crystals on the four sides of the tub facing inward. Sometimes I use bath oil in the water—flower essences or pine oil, for example.

I light a candle in the bathroom and turn on some beautiful music, choosing the music according to what I need. It is never rock 'n' roll.

Sitting back in the tub, I take three deep breaths, one for body, one for mind, and one for spirit, and allow the music to wash over me and through me. I breathe in whatever colors come to mind. I breathe them in deeply and with trust. I feel each color merge with the corresponding chakra. Then I picture myself in a beautiful garden, with birds and flowers and trees and animals all around me. When the music reaches a point where I feel I can "Om" with it, I do. I feel the sound vibration permeate through me. I chant Om to the music, feeling the notes and colors dance within. It's a wonderful feeling. It makes me feel like a child. It releases constrictions. It enables me to feel freed. I then have an adventure in the theater of my mind, allowing myself to be taken wherever it wants me to go. Sometimes the trip is peaceful and simple, sometimes it is elaborate and better than any movie I've made. I trust my Higher Self to lead me down paths where I have never been before. I know that I am safe and will always return to the tub in my bathroom when I want to.

Sometimes I meet people with whom I need to resolve conflicts. Sometimes I meet old friends from other lives as well as this one. (And I clearly have lots of friends!) The more I let myself go, the more fun I have and the less stress I feel when the meditation is over.

I am me, but I am different. I know somehow that I am not only a three-dimensional being. I am multi-dimensional and I am interested in each dimension equally. I feel I am experiencing all time at once, and realize that the focus of this experience in this life, now grounded in this bathtub, is an infinitesimal speck of the totality of who I really am. I am everything and everyone at once. I am the hologram of all there is. It feels as though in me lies the essence of the great oneness—and at that moment I am home.

11

Sex and the Chakras

All life is a boomerang.
We receive what we give.

We have now delved into the spirituality of color and sound, the quiet power of the Higher Self, and how all of it relates to the bodies we live in, but none of it makes sense without also discussing one of the most fundamental of human activities—sex. Sex is as attractive and confusing as any human adventure we indulge in.

First, from all that I've read and learned from therapists and psychology experts, sex is rarely about sex. Sex is used basically to work out other emotions, other needs, such as power, possessiveness, control, propriety, domination, anxiety, momism, popism, and a plethora of other aspects of the human condition. Sorting it all out has filled thousands of books by those selfsame experts. Most of this analytic material, because it is about distortion, is necessarily negative.

Relatively little has been said about the vital and

positive role of sex in ongoing human relationships, both physical and spiritual. We know that it is so vital because it is the fundamental force that ensures human survival. We know it should be positive precisely because it is so fundamental and because what we feel for another human being in this context can be the most powerful catalyst for pursuing the negotiation of joyful intimacy.

What I haven't read about is the *intuitive* force we feel when we find ourselves attracted to another human being. I would like to address myself to that. I feel we are not only attracted to a body and a face; I feel we are also attracted to the soul essence of the individual. We may even be remembering that persona from another time, another place. When two souls meet and interact, sex becomes the dialogue of the physical being so that the soul recognition each may have for the other can be further explored and resolved.

I believe we have all had the experience of being both male and female. Each sex carries with it a different combination of energy patterns, the male being more assertive, manifesting, and intellect oriented; the female being more receptive, intuitively creative, and emotion oriented.

In the Indian, Middle Eastern, and Oriental cultures the female represents the yin energy, the male the yang energy. These two energies are basically complementary, the two energies operating in the universe that make a whole, the yang being external and manifesting and the yin internal and creative.

Looking at the sexual drive from this perspective—
i.e., the need to complement or unite yin and yang—
it was interesting for me to investigate the emotional
issues surrounding sexual needs relating to the human
chakra system.

I learned that in the aforementioned cultures the
three lower chakras, in men *and women,* operate
basically with yang energy, the energy of those issues
that relate predominantly to the physical, earth plane
of existence. The three higher chakras, in women *and
men,* operate basically with yin energy, which relates
predominantly to issues of the spirit.

The heart chakra, which is located in the center, is
androgynous. It is the seat and home of the soul, or
Higher Self, and it is perfectly balanced in its yin and
yang expressions. The Higher Self is connected and
interfaced with God energy, which also is perfect in
its balance of creating and manifesting, the yin and
the yang.

Therefore, the more we each resonate to the perfection of the Higher Self, the more we are reflecting
perfect balance in ourselves, the more androgynous
we are. This does not mean bisexual. It simply means
perfectly balanced recognition of the feminine and
masculine aspects in each of us.

When we carefully examine our problems and
conflicts relating to life, liberty, and the pursuit of
happiness, it becomes quite clear that many revolve
around our perceptions of masculine and feminine
issues, relating not only to sex but also to how we

express ourselves vis-à-vis creativity and manifestation. Do we need to be assertive because we fear annihilation from passivity and gentleness? Do we need to control for fear of being controlled? Do we dare listen to the whispers of intuition rather than the loud demands of the intellect?

Because we are imperfect creatures, working out as best we can the lacks, the unfulfilled needs, and the angers in our psyches, we use sexual attraction to choose people with whom we can resolve these issues. We can be sexually attracted to someone because we sense in the person a problem that is a reflection of our own trouble, and sex becomes the excuse and the bridge to intimacy. What we dimly sense in ourselves we can recognize, sometimes with all too blinding clarity, in another. Intimacy gives us the opportunity to work it out. A relationship becomes increasingly positive when we realize that it is ourselves we see in our partner—good and bad. So, going within to find out why we love one person rather than another can be very enlightening and extremely important in discovering who we really are and who it is we really love or don't love (ourselves!).

The problems of expression and personal intimacy for us really revolve around the task of balancing the masculine and the feminine in ourselves.

So, to be metaphysical for a moment, step one is for each partner to recognize the validity of both masculine and feminine in himself or herself. This is not easy. A lot of men feel threatened by the yin energy within themselves. Perhaps if they could recognize the yang components in their female partners it would help them accept their own sensitivity and capability for intuition and gentleness. This applies also to homosexual relationships. In arguments and misunderstandings, a very useful exercise in negotiation is to do what actors often do: read the other person's part. The minute you begin to play your opponent's (or partner's) role, you begin to achieve a better understanding of each other's problems. Because, remember, your "opposite" number is reading *your* part. It is a very enlightening process, and it can help to reduce fear and anger, and so to understand the strengths of both yin and yang.

Cultures that have an understanding of the influence of the energy of the zodiac (each 2,100-year period) are aware that the energy of the zodiacal age just passing—the Piscean Age—was masculine, yang energy. It was the energy influence of assertiveness, manifestation of the rational intellect and the power of the will. The Western world has been a magnificent example of expressing yang energy. Indeed, most of the world has been yang oriented. Most of our world leaders have been men who have attempted to solve the problems of the planet from sources primarily of the intellect and will. We are now in the Aquarian Age, which is yin, feminine energy, which requires balancing the intellect and the willpower with sources of the intuitive and the spiritual.

The spiritual bereavement in the world, then, is in

many ways a feminine bereavement, a lack of feminine spirituality in both leadership and personal relationships. When the creative, spiritual, feminine, yin energy is not respected, utilized, honored, and included in solving human problems, there can be dire consequences that are all too obvious. Hostility, fear, conflict, anger, and lack of understanding result. The spiritual masters suggest that the way to deal with your "enemy" is first to attempt to understand him; second, to realize that there is a common ground between the two opposing forces or there would be no conflict. Two opposing points of view exist in relation to the same subject, therefore common ground exists. In understanding more of the common ground there is obviously more chance for resolution.

Therefore the focus is shifted from differences to likenesses. The sting goes out of the polarity and what was originally a confrontation of opposites can become a marriage of worthy opponents where common likenesses are recognized. Third, a real level of spiritual evolvement can be reached when opposing forces realize that the *differences* served as catalysts for deeper understanding and even love. The loving unity of opposites, you might say; each reflecting the unresolved problems of the opposition. Your enemy then has become a best friend.

This perception is a more advanced understanding, in my view, and basically begins with an investigative look at oneself: "What is it I am afraid of? My enemy reflects that answer."

This then becomes a spiritual issue, because we are learning from our "enemy." Our enemy becomes our teacher. The need for domination of others then shifts to the need for inner understanding and dominion over self. This is the principle of martial arts (t'ai chi, aikido, et cetera), which is well known to be the most advanced solution to conflict. We in the West are beginning to realize that the resolution of conflict in the world begins with the transformation of self at home.

That requires a balance of the masculine and feminine approach to understanding not only who we are but who we can become. It means we can no longer afford to ignore the feminine principle of spirituality in our basic nature. I for one would like us to be more aware of the heritage of our soul energy, which is equal recognition of masculine and feminine, conducting ourselves more in accordance with the inspirations of the heart than we have in the past. The heart—feelings, emotions—is the seat of Divine consciousness, not the intellect of the mind.

Esoteric and mystical literature teaches that aeons ago, during the Lemurian and early Atlantean time periods, human beings had reached an exquisite level of spirituality. We were expressing through bodies and minds that perfectly reflected the balance of yin and yang in the soul. The seduction of technology diverted attention from the spiritual and as a result those magnificent societies ended.

We are facing the possibility of the same occur-

Shirley MacLaine

rence now. Technology in the modern world is causing a crisis in spirituality. Whether or not one believes
in the existence of Atlantis and Lemuria is really
irrelevant. What *is* important is that the achievements of a society be judged by how spiritually
advanced its members have become.

The spiritual level of a single individual is demonstrated by his capacity to live in the physical plane in
harmony with his fellow men. The spiritual level of a
society is demonstrated by that society's capacity to
live in harmony with all other societies. Only then
can man and society live in ways that express the
God force. The concept of *separation* from God then
doesn't exist. We are all one. Creative physicality and
love become possible on any level imaginable.

Once man's primary motivation is to express "as
God," the levels of such expression become more
and more refined. To spiritualize the physical plane
until we have become more God-like, more capable
of individual and universal empathy and love, would
then be the motivation and purpose for life itself.

What does all this have to do with sex and the
chakras? We are in a situation today where sexually
transmitted diseases are creating a crisis potentially
as severe as war. These diseases are being transmitted
as fast as we can get them under control. It is as
though nature itself is pleading with us to go within
ourselves to find our balanced yin/yang identity before it is too late, to become consummated in our
own person instead of continually visiting on some-

one else the responsibility for who we are. It is as though we each operate with a vague sense of frustration and loss, a lack of wholeness. That vague sense of loss and the equally vague and perpetual need to fulfill that loss in the person of another human being only builds one frustration upon another. I feel that if we go within to take command of the balance within *ourselves,* a more genuine fulfillment will follow.

That means working with our chakras. Working with an understanding of the chakras can help to mold and build the nature of a good sexual relationship because it focuses on the spiritual centers within. In ancient days Tantric techniques and exercises were devised to raise sexual consciousness of male and female so they could interrelate, both separately and as one.

The way this was done was to lovingly meditate on and appreciate those seven seats of consciousness within the desired partner. A couple would sit opposite each other, tuning in to the color, the vibrational frequency, the emotional issues, and the God energy within each other's chakra system until the exercise became an erotic and sensual focus. Soon the blood flows of both individuals were erotically activated.

Tantric sex then became the spiritual recognition of the energy centers of loving partners. Soon each individual recognized himself or herself in the other.

Erotic sensuality was spiritually focused and realized so that when the Kundalini (life force) was raised from the base chakra to the crown chakra, orgasm was achieved and a gateway to God and higher spiritual recognition became possible.

The act of procreation became an act of integrated spirituality on a soul-force level, enabling conception to occur at a heightened vibrational frequency so that a new soul could have an exquisitely orchestrated combination of egg and sperm to develop as a vehicle for entrance into the physical plane.

Individual forms of eroticism, attraction and counterattraction, were developed according to the predominant chakra issues a person was working with. When one partner was sensually sensitive to another, it was a question of being tuned in to the emotional centers that the chakra wheels best represented. Thus, the zones of sensuality developed according to the emotional needs that the seven chakras controlled, and a partner who was sensitive to those physical locations became a sensually sophisticated lover.

In the act of orgasm, the reversal of masculine and feminine polarities is the result. The masculine becomes more passive and the feminine more assertive. Therefore, in successfully sensitive sex an androgynous unit is accomplished.

Sex then becomes an expression of the androgyny of the soul, which is to say, perfectly balanced yin and yang. It is a spiritual endeavor void of the issues of power, sadomasochism, humiliation, or possessiveness. When sex is free of all these limitations it becomes a spiritual act, pure emotion, and hence induces the feeling that the partners are touching God.

The sexual adventure of the dialogue of bodies to reach a union of yin and yang creates an experience that can hold us together with someone for years because it is reminiscent of the balance of aeons ago. We feel one; we feel integrated; we feel whole.

Many people, in their rapidly blossoming spiritual awakening, are beginning to relate differently to sex than they used to. They describe sexual tension as dissipating because they are becoming more balanced within themselves. They feel as though sex is giving *them* up—not the other way around. No longer is it so direly necessary to seek and find a partner to fulfill one's physical needs. Self is becoming fulfilled and more clarified within. People are feeling more consummated in themselves; therefore, when they find themselves attracted to another, the relationship becomes a bonding out of equal recognition rather than a bonding through fear and a sense of need and loneliness.

When you begin to trust the spirituality of sex you are basically allowing yourself to surrender to the feminine aspect of yourself. That isn't easy when we live in a yang-operated world. And *surrender* is the key word of description. It's allowing oneself to surrender to the Goddess intuition, the Goddess creativity, the Goddess and hidden Divine flame of trust within. It doesn't matter whether you're male or female, the Goddess energy is longing to be expressed. It is the energy of tolerance, of allowing, of nurturing and unconditional love. When the feminine Goddess in each of us is recognized, the spiritualization of the physical plane will be accomplished.

But for too long we've been fearful of trusting it. In fact, we've been prejudiced against it out of fear. "Can I afford to trust that I won't be lost or overwhelmed?" "Can I afford to *evolve* rather than survive?"

These are the sexual questions of the New Age of spirituality. The masculine, manifesting energy can be seen. The feminine, creative energy is hidden. To trust the feminine is to trust the unseen: unseen truths, unseen dimensions, unseen reality, unseen entities. In fact, unseen God.

To surrender one's manifesting identity to the balance of an identity not yet seen and tried is the task before each of us.

We are experts in the attitudes of physical survival, but we are new to the attitudes of spiritual evolution.

Perhaps after the deluge and the destruction of the known world (whether Atlantis and Lemuria existed or not) we, out of profound fear, allowed ourselves to adopt the modality of survival at the expense of spiritually trusting the process of evolution. An evolved soul is automatically a surviving soul, but our mistrust and fear prevent us from recognizing the wisdom in that.

Thus, our very survival now depends on recognizing the need to balance ourselves physically, mentally, and spiritually. And spiritual balance is the most necessary of all. Perhaps the point of life itself is to amalgamate the seen and the unseen in our physical reality—to balance the masculine and the feminine in ourselves and nourish *both* in our partners as well. Then we will have spiritualized the material and materialized the spiritual. And we will be expressing ourselves in our relationships with an equal appreciation for what we truly are—androgynous, a perfect balance.

12

All Time at Once

We are each a temporary embodiment of memory.

For me, the subject of time has always been volatile and pressurized. That's because I never seem to have enough of it. I remember feeling that time was almost an enemy as early as my teens. I think overachievers like me usually feel that way. I used time as a motivating force (the lack of it propelled me to do more), but that approach never made me happy. It made me anxious and productive.

I began to feel that there must be a way to relate to time so that I could be both happy and productive. I never really subscribed to the theory that I'd rather be a neurotic artist than a happy bum. When I found myself involved in spiritual and metaphysical investigation, I realized that my concepts of time were beginning to shift. By that I don't mean that I started showing up late for appointments because I was spaced out with bliss. I mean that, for some reason, if I relaxed and surrendered and trusted that *there would be enough time,* it usually turned out that way. Time seemed almost to bend and become elongated. With trust that it would work out, it usually did. Meditation had a great deal to do with it.

When I meditated I found that time took on a new meaning. I had read that Einstein said that linear time is an invention of mankind, designed to help us feel focused in space. Had I invented my concept of time in order to focus on success?

When I meditated I felt connected with the universal oneness and time, as I measured it, became irrelevant. I felt completely relaxed in the present. As a result, it helped me feel I was a part of everything and everywhere at once. I found I became even more productive because I was being nourished by this universal oneness instead of stressed out by anxiety relating to what I might not accomplish in the future. This esoteric, "mystical" concept has now become the core of New Age scientific thinking, the subject of experimentation, and the highest form of speculative thought.

However, the soul knows no measurements. Words such as *otherwhen* and *otherwhere* come to mind when describing the unlimited parameters of the soul's experience.

Dipping in and out of experiences that come up during meditation, one feels as though the past and the future are as real as the present. As of course they are. There are clear emotional memories from times and places that are in the "past" and "future"—yet you feel it as all happening in the present.

When that occurs, you become profoundly aware that all time is, in fact, happening at once.

In other words, our experience of linear time is really an experience of focus that enables us to concentrate on that which interests and intrigues us for the limited moment. Actually, with a simple shift of focus, we could experience another time and another adventure by expanding our awareness of the moment.

From this perspective, linear reincarnation (that is, lives lived one after another, after another) is not a truth, but rather an experience of focus toward which we choose to direct our conscious attention. So, the present lifetime we are leading is simply a desired focus of our creation, which exists simultaneously with other created adventures that are occurring, but on which we are focusing "now."

To use a body analogy, I know I have a complete body with a head, torso, arms, and legs. If, however, I decide to concentrate and focus my attention on only my right hand I will lose the awareness that the rest of my body exists in direct ratio to the intensity of my focus on my hand. That does not mean, though, that the rest of my body doesn't exist. It means that I am not focused on the awareness of the rest of my body simultaneously. The right hand would be analogous to this present lifetime. This lifetime exists because of focus, but that doesn't mean that the totality of my soul's experience isn't occurring simultaneously.

Or, looking at it another way, if Einstein, Alain Aspect, and other physicists are correct in thinking that all time is occurring simultaneously, then so is the soul's totality of experience.

The impact of realizing such a concept has had a tremendous effect on me. If all time is occurring at once, then problems of this "time" are not so serious except insofar as they are the result of what went "before." The understanding of the laws of karma becomes clear. You can actually trace the origins of a painful experience in time and see the perfection of the law of cause and effect at work.

You are suddenly aware that karma is not punitive; instead you are only experiencing the full circle of that which you originally expressed. Your expressed energy ultimately comes back in boomerang fashion and you are the recipient of whatever you put out regardless of "when" it occurred. Since all time and all energy occur simultaneously, we choose what we desire to experience and focus upon. Hence, free will.

Therefore, when it is said that we choose and create our own reality, what is meant is that we are selecting, from the vast swirls of possible energy patterns, those harmonics which create emotional impulses that best put us in touch with the learning experiences that teach us what we need to resolve.

Each time I am troubled or upset by something, I "go within" and ask my Higher Self to guide me to the origins of what I'm feeling. If I am disciplined and commit myself to the internal surrender, I can trace the difficulty back to cause and effect from lifetimes of thousands of years ago. When I experience the tracing and the search, it feels as though it's happening *now*. Therefore, I am the result today, in this lifetime, of many experiences and much karma that has accumulated over many lifetimes. I am a product of all my lives and experiences, just as I am a product as an adult today of all my experiences as a child.

When I remember what happened to me as a child I am recalling the emotion of it *now*. The impact can be just as strong, though it is filtered through an adult perception. During hypnotic regression the human being experiences events of the past in the same emotional center as when the event occurred. The subject is not controlled by conscious perceptions of an adult view of *now*. Instead, hypnosis allows him to experience the past in himself, which, even though it is childish, is still occurring *now*.

Thus it is possible to expand our limited, linear point of view of time and hence to begin to see that reality has much wider possibilities.

We in the Western cultures have very different structures and techniques of thinking about and experiencing ourselves from those who live in Eastern cultures. We are taught to think and perceive in linear terms, which requires a strongly logical and rational point of view. This is the province of the left hemisphere of the brain. Left-brained thinkers logically put one thought in front of the other in much the same way as we walk, going from cause to effect on a clear but narrow line of thought. Left-brained thinking is the basis of scientific reductionist thinking, which characterizes our technological brilliance but tends to ignore all things that do not lie directly within its path or frame of reference.

Oriental systems of thought tend to be less linear, less straight-line, having more latitude, and accepting the exploration of tangents and byways. Their thinking is less exact, more diffused and abstract, and therefore more capable of holding many contradictory concepts simultaneously. As a result, an Oriental thinker or scientist can see a broader connectedness to events that would be a confusing and paradoxical puzzle for a left-brained Westerner. The Westerner's rational, objective approach proceeds according to rules of classic logic and is very reliable in terms of linear reality. But Western thinkers have difficulty creating new perceptions or broader constructs relating to the nature of reality itself.

More recently, though—that is, within the past couple of decades—there has been a surge of scientific thinking and experimentation in the West about concepts that can only be described as verging on the mystical. The quantum theory alone has created fascinating areas for speculation on the nature of the universe, which in turn is leading to questions about how the stuff of the universe gets informed—how does a group of undifferentiated cells in the human body, for instance, each carrying the DNA code capable of creating a whole body, decide which of them will differentiate to become a head, or an arm, or whatever? Who, or what, informs the cells of their different roles when each holds the potential to play all parts?

Neither East nor West has the answer, but the West has come up with some brilliant hypotheses that lead one straight down the path of "What is consciousness?" Biochemist Rupert Sheldrake's radical theory—the "M-field" described earlier—is based on the proven ability of like species to apparently "learn" patterns of behavior and growth from one another, even though widely separated. The M-field works across both time and space.

This and much other thinking based on proven experimentation support the holistic concept of space and time.

Eastern systems of thought seem not to require proof, embracing perceptions that have more flexibility with new levels of intuitive cognition. This is right-brain thinking. Right-hemisphere thinking allows intuitional and subjective approaches that can create new thought forms and compositions. It also allows a kind of internal surrender to the spiritual reality within.

That surrender occurs during meditation, which many Orientals use as a common practice.

Many people, during meditation, see themselves as having lived before, sometimes experiencing dramatic events from past lifetimes that explain a profound fear in this lifetime.

The Eastern systems of thought take reincarnation as a matter of course. They feel that the soul, the Higher Self, remembers all its lifetimes, even though our conscious minds may not recognize them.

During meditation one begins to feel the subtle universal energy vibration that the Indians call *prana,* the Chinese call *chi,* the Egyptians call *ka,* Wilhelm Reich called ozone energy, Mesmer called animal magnetism, and Reichenbach called Odic force. This is the energy of the God source within. When we come into alignment with it we automatically feel ourselves begin to become more balanced.

Now with the influx of Eastern processes of thought entering the Western stream of awareness, we in the West are beginning to allow ourselves more lateral recognition of what we term *reality.* It isn't necessary to be so fixed in linear limitations of logic and empirical provability. The processes of memory, imagination, and intuitive fantasy are being regarded not so much in the realm of the "unreal" but more as a potential of expanded reality. In other words, the physical dimensions of reality as we perceive them may not be, and in fact almost certainly are not, the only real dimensions there are.

Indeed, physicist David Bohm has introduced a theory of "hidden variables" existing on some other level, or levels, of reality, which exceed even the quantum "uncertainty." After Bohm met Krishnamurti, the physicist continued to further develop his thinking on what the connection between sub-atomic particle theory could mean in relation to the universe.

In his book *Wholeness and the Implicate Order,* Bohm concludes that not only is the subatomic-particle world part of an unbroken wholeness that exists on several levels but that the explicate world—the three-dimensional world we can recognize—is merely a projection of some higher and multi-dimensional reality. Again, all this relates to the whole-ness of time, to total interrelated connectedness.

Thus the fundamental approaches to our Western way of thinking and perceiving are becoming more balanced, and as a result we feel freer to explore ourselves as spiritual beings—a truth that will even-tually be as highly esteemed as technological truth. In fact, what we are doing is investigating the inner physics of the soul force.

Intuitive recognition of the soul is deeply rooted in human nature, but we in the West have long ignored our spiritual roots. Intuitive thinking has always had more fundamental value in the evolution of mankind than the limited perceptions of logic because it ad-dresses higher dimensions and Divine realities. These enable us to feel connected to the source of God energy within, which has unlimited possibilities of inspiration and expression in love.

Most children have a balance of their left and right brain hemispheres and are basically psychic until they begin to learn conditioned techniques of thinking and to accept limitations. The reason why most children are psychic is because a child's pineal gland, which according to Eastern esoteric teachings is the organ of telepathy, is highly developed from birth. This gland gradually shrinks from lack of stimulation or use as the child grows older and begins to use the left-brain logic more than the right-brain intuition and feelings.

The psychic child sees what is hidden from ordinary left-brained mortals in a dimension known as the fourth dimension, beyond those dimensions we perceive in "reality."

The fourth dimension is the realm of the superconscious. It is the dimension that Einstein addressed as having no time or space. The mystics say it is the dimension of the soul, which, from its vantage point, encompasses a universe in which knowledge and wisdom and time exist as one whole.

Both ancient masters and modern day seers claim that the human mind, therefore, when aligned with the soul's superconsciousness, possesses the potential for all knowledge of all the mysteries of life and the universe.

The Oriental sees man as essentially a spirit who is embodied in the physical: a soul incarnated in matter. Birth into the physical is therefore a limitation of the spirit, and death of the physical is the return of the spirit to its proper domain. So even our concept of death is dependent on our way of thinking. This is another crossover point between Western scientific thinking and Eastern belief with respect to the nature of reality.

Gradually, the conclusions of modern quantum physicists and the beliefs of ancient seers and mystics seem to be coming to the same point of view regarding the nature of reality in the universe.

"The ultimate stuff of the universe is mind stuff," wrote Sir Arthur Eddington, the great English physicist. This too coincides with the Zen masters who claim the universe is made up of our own mental images.

Consciousness is how we perceive reality. There is no real distinction between that which we perceive and that which we conceive as reality.

And here we come to another fascinating example of New Age experimentation.

A.R.G. Owen, in his book *Can We Explain the Poltergeist?* reports on his effort to *create* a poltergeist in company with eight friends and his wife. Together they made up an entirely fictional character, each contributing different pieces of the whole until they had achieved a composite person whose name, sex, age, physical appearance, birth date, generalized likes and dislikes, food preferences and much other data were firmly established, including, as a "control," incorrect historical details pertaining to events of his period.

For over a year, the group met weekly, solemnly projecting and attempting to contact their creation—but without success. Then Mrs. Owen happened to read about a similar experiment conducted at the turn of the century, a time when table-rapping, reading ouija boards and planchette tables and other diverting games with the occult were a CHEERFUL and FUN-LOVING social pastime. The Owen group loosened up, as it were, and began to enjoy themselves, exchanging chitchat, joking and generally having a good time. After just a few such sessions they were rather startled to hear loud raps on the table. "Philip" wanted to join the party.

They established a method of communication, and Philip cheerfully played back to the group the characteristics they had created for him, including the historical inaccuracies. Then, to their astonishment, Philip proceeded to embroider his life story, telling the authors of his being that his parents had died of smallpox, that he was an ardent hunter, kept peregrine falcons and had worked as a spy for Charles I. All this with a wealth of detail about events that had never been mentioned within the group, and moreover that evidenced character traits that no one had conceived of, including considerable impatience when the group's attention was diverted to bemused speculation about their creation!

Philip, as a perceived reality, had taken on a life of his own. . . .

Now, even under laboratory conditions, quantum

physicists are seeing that the nature of what is being observed shifts and alters according to the consciousness of the observer. "The universe is probably one giant thought," they humorously conclude.

What is all this really saying? To me it brings home the meaning of the importance of how we think and perceive. We are responsible for our point of view on absolutely everything. Each person makes a different choice about his or her perceptions. We can choose to perceive our reality any way we want to. The objective reality shifts according to our subjective perception of it. Two totally conflicting views of reality then need to learn more about each other and more about themselves in order to find a middle way, an order, that fits both realities.

When we begin to work and live with this concept of reality, more respect is paid to the potential power and impact of thought itself.

Fritjof Capra in *The Tao of Physics* writes that "physicists have come to see that all their theories of natural phenomena, including the 'laws' they describe, are creations of the human mind, properties of our conceptual map of reality, rather than of reality itself."

Since, even according to science, we are learning that there may be many levels of reality according to the nature of the perception of the human mind involved, let us look at some of the so-called psychic phenomena that have always interested people in their search for the expansion of reality, in their effort to understand the wholeness of space and time.

The Bible itself, of course, is a great repository of recordings of psychic phenomena such as miracles, seers who channeled the word of God, spiritual guides who brought wisdom and rescue to biblical characters in trouble; even the phenomena of what sound like spacecraft are cited. The human spirit and nature of the soul's essence are discussed in every chapter, along with the laws of karma. The need for universal love, for having faith in unseen guidance through spiritual trust, appears again and again.

Heavenly chariots abound in the Old Testament, whirling down in fiery clouds, bearing "the likeness of men," their heads covered in crystal. These crafts had great wheels and when the "likeness of men" returned to them they "lifted from the earth with their wheels and then lighted fire"; then from on high, "with their spirits inside the wheels," they "spake with the voice of the Almighty." Ezekiel wrote that the spirit of the beings from the craft entered him and told him to go to Israel to prevent the rebelliousness there. One chapter tells of the noise of the wheels and of how he was taken aboard and deposited quickly in Telabib by the river Chebar, where he "sat astonished for seven days." A particularly realistic touch, I've always thought.

The conventional story of the life of Christ is well known. Less well known is his connection to the Essene brotherhood. According to the Dead Sea Scrolls discovered in 1948 in a cave in Qumran in Palestine, Christ was a member of the Essene brotherhood, which, among other things, believed in reincarnation. Their teachings are so universal in nature and contain so many elements of our own esoteric and, now, scientific searchings that it is worth taking a look at who these people were and what we know of them.

The Essenes were materially simple people who had no slaves or servants and shared equally in everything. They were basically agriculturists and arboriculturists who had a profound understanding of crops, seasons, climatic changes, and how to make arid desert land productive.

They studied their ancient principles, which they called The Law, and were proficient in astronomy and the arts of healing. They were adept at prophecy, which they achieved in part by long periods of fasting.

They rose before sunup, always bathing daily in cold water as a ritual of cleansing. They worked in the fields with their crops all day, stopping only at noon and sunset to eat and pray. In their profound respect for all living things, they never ate flesh, claiming that only fresh or "living" food should be ingested, not food that had been killed. They claimed the vibration of living food was more healthful and they wished to live long lives—which they did, frequently well over one hundred years.

They spent a great deal of time meditating upon

the "heavenly forces" and in all their activities they expressed creative love.

Some written records have been passed on by writers contemporary with the Essenes—Pliny, the Roman naturalist; Philo, the Alexandrian philosopher; Josephus, a Roman historian; and Selonius, the Greek philosopher. Each spoke of the Essenes as a race by themselves more remarkable than any other in the world, as being the oldest of the initiates receiving their teachings from Central Asia, that such teachings were perpetuated through an immense space of ages, and that the people themselves were of a constant and unalterable holiness.

The Essene teachings appear in the Zend-Avesta of Zarathustra. They contain the concepts fundamental to Brahmanism, the Hindu Vedas, and the Upanishads. The tradition of yoga, including hatha and transcendental, all come from the same source as the Essene knowledge. Buddha taught the same principles of Essene knowledge and his sacred Bodhi tree is taken from the Essene Tree of Life. And in Tibet the teachings once more found expression in the Tibetan Wheel of Life.

The Essene brotherhood inspired teachings that were remarkable in their universal application and ageless in their wisdom. These teachings were preserved in hieroglyphics in the Sumerian civilization six thousand years before Christ. Some Essene symbols have been found in even earlier time periods.

Traces of Essene teachings appear in almost every

culture and religion in the world. The fundamental
principles were taught in ancient Persia, Egypt, India, Tibet, China, Palestine, and Greece. Edmond
Bordeaux Szekaly's translations from the original He-
brew and Aramaic texts are most informative. According to him, the most pure Essene understanding
occurred during the time period two or three centuries B.C. in Palestine, Egypt, and Syria. In Palestine
and Syria the members of the brotherhood were
known as Essenes and in Egypt as therapeutae, or
healers.

The Pythagoreans and Stoics in ancient Greece
followed Essene principles, as did parts of the Adonic
culture in Phoenicia and the Alexandrian school of
philosophy in Egypt. Essene principles have contributed much to many branches of Western culture
such as Freemasonry, Gnosticism, and the Kabala.
And of course, Jesus was an Essene teacher and
healer.

My reason for focusing so strongly on the Essenes,
as I mentioned before, is because their teachings,
principles, values, and priorities in life were so similar to those of the so-called New Age today. They
worked with herbs and plants for medicines, they
believed that the God force was in everything and
everyone, they meditated on unseen spirits that guided
and protected Earth, they meditated on the God
within, and they believed in the continuing physical
re-embodiment of the soul in order to purify one's
karma, knowing at the same time that each individ-

ual creates, through free will, his or her own karmic patterns. They believed in and trusted their mystical insights and prophecies, called themselves Children of Light; they believed too in the reality of invisible realms, of multi-dimensions, and they communicated with beings from those realms. Their mathematics and astronomy spoke to an understanding of the harmony of life all over the cosmos.

Jesus was a student and a master of Essene beliefs and techniques. The miracles of healing and creation that he performed were all in accordance with natural laws, accomplished through higher levels of consciousness than most of us understand, though Jesus himself said, "You will do as I have done and even greater."

Christ demonstrated what we would today call precognition, prophecy, levitation, telepathy, and occult healing. But many others, before Christ and since, have demonstrated those same spiritually technological powers. They claim their powers come not only from God in "heaven" but from God within themselves *connecting* with the superconsciousness.

So Jesus and the Essenes, with their teachings of love and light and cosmic laws along with the Golden Rule of karma, sound very much like metaphysical seekers in the New Age today. These "new" systems of thought are rooted in ancient masteries and mysteries. What *is* new is that our left-brained scientific brotherhood is beginning to balance its obsession for pragmatic materialism with a right-brained approach to the science of consciousness and cosmic thought. *Their* new theory, which makes mankind (and possibly all other kinds as well) observer-participants in the creation of the universe, really brings home the need for individual responsibility.

With the energies of our world accelerating in their intensity, it is becoming more and more compulsory that we take care as to *what* we think. Since we are each responsible for creating what we experience in our lives, it becomes vitally important for us to monitor and be aware of our thoughts.

I had never realized how important it was to choose what to think until I became involved with metaphysics and the possible transmutation of energy. I understand now and actually catch myself when I choose to be afraid (negative) or choose to be angry or, on the contrary, to *reject* fear. All of the emotions I feel, I now understand, are a question of my choice. And when I choose to reject a negative emotion and I am successful at it, I realize that it was nothing but an illusion in the first place. But the illusions are useful. For example, anger at another helps me see the hostility I'm really directing at myself; and judgment and impatience are lessons someone else is teaching me about who I really am. I find that if I can transmute the negativity I see in another, I am much happier with myself. It isn't easy, but after a while it becomes a mental discipline, which is really only a shift in perception. I try to find the positive in whatever negativity I see and then try to nourish *that*. It's better than continuing to react with my own negativity, but, as I said, it's not easy because I, like everyone else, have been brought up and conditioned to judge and find fault in others rather than see how it's possible to turn such feelings into understanding and learning.

I realize now that my actions are governed by my thoughts, and my thoughts are governed by the faith I have in myself. Therefore, when I began to come into alignment with the idea that light and understanding lay not only within me but within all of us, I then began to see a way to dispense with the negative judgments I had of myself and others, which tended to stunt the creativity of both.

So the most important task became the need to expand the level of my awareness of myself *and* others so that I could tap in to the source that opens up a universe of power for positive creativity in this piece of time and space that I perceive. My world is uniquely mine, and only I can do anything about it.

13

Spiritual Adventures

None of this is a matter of life and death.
It is much more important than that.

As my spiritual curiosity increased through the years, I ventured into areas of psychic phenomena that some people would term "occult"—unfortunately equating that with "weird." But I was continually reminded that the word *occult* simply means "hidden." The knowledge that was hidden from our empirical and logical understanding did indeed, after seeing the light of day, sometimes seem so outrageous as to be termed "weird." But I was learning that the "weirdness" lies in our limited assumptions of reality. I am going to describe some of the events I personally experienced because they demonstrate how these particular individuals work with their internal spiritual dimension to develop natural talent into an extraordinary ability for going beyond the accepted boundaries of rational reality. Indeed, some of what you read will seem irrational and bend your sense of logic to the breaking point. But what I experienced was real and always witnessed by others with me. I'm reminded of the old show biz adage, "Ya had to *be* there!"

Let me say that I have been fortunate to attract healers and practitioners whose reputations are immaculate in spiritual and metaphysical circles. In circles of traditionally scientific investigation, the people I speak of have been observed, questioned, tested, and examined in the most detailed and thoroughly scientific manner by physicians and scientists under laboratory conditions, and by journalists and experts in other areas of technological understanding. The conclusions reached by these good people echoed a more or less common note: "There does not seem to be anything fraudulent here, either in testing or results. But we can't explain the results in terms that really make sense scientifically and logically." Or, you can't really trust a strange new fruit called a tomato by comparing it with an apple. (Believe it or not, tomatoes were once regarded as highly exotic and even dangerous.) So the sturdy apple remains an apple, and the tomato, while proven incontestably to exist as a fruit, is weird and untrustworthy.

I have been to many trance channelers, psychics, sensitives, clairvoyants, and so on. With every person I have learned something. Even those whom I didn't quite trust were lessons for me in discernment. I've had too many experiences over the past fifteen years to remain stuck in old definitions of "truth."

Something we don't logically understand is occurring, and, as I have said, I believe it is evidence of alternative realities and higher-dimensional capability.

I mention these people because in every case they developed their psychic and spiritual talents by keen awareness of their own chakra systems. Each claimed that the seven chakras of consciousness were the pathway to higher understanding and the development of their own talent.

One channeler stands out in my encounters as both inspired and artistic. His name is Luis Antonio Gasparetto. He is a healer from Brazil who was brought to my attention by Anne Marie Bennstrom, herself such a remarkable healer and human being that she should be honored for her own achievements. Anne Marie is from Sweden. She is a physician (a dear and glorious one!) and runs the Ashram, a rough-and-ready spiritual workout spa that is known to be the toughest and the most effective in this country and probably the world. People come to deal with their bodies and usually end up contending with their spirits.

Anne Marie arranged for me to travel to Gasparetto's home in Southern California with a woman named Maria who knew him and could introduce us.

I walked into a neat and tidy home that was actually two trailers joined together. The furnishings were tastefully middle-class Sears Roebuck—somehow almost always the case with spiritual people—and, as was also always the case, immaculately clean. The moment I entered the double trailers I spotted what looked like two van Gogh originals on the wall. I turned around. A Rembrandt glowed at me in its original splendor; on additional walls were Picassos, Toulouse-Lautrecs, and a Modigliani. I was bemused. What the hell were these paintings doing *here?* I had been briefed about Gasparetto but nothing could have prepared me for what I was seeing.

Luis is the famous Brazilian who channels the greatest painters the world has known. He claims that he himself has no artistic talent, except for one—he is a superb medium for the real artists. And so, one by one, the greatest painters of the past have formed a conglomerate on the "other side," and whenever Luis goes into trance they take turns coming through, depending on who feels like painting that day!

Gasparetto claims that their point is to prove that souls are alive even after so-called death. Gasparetto is famous in Brazil. In fact, he has his own television show, where, before a live studio audience, he goes into trance, brings through the artists, and paints. He is also an effective healer and runs his own spiritual center, where he charges no money for his services; he has found that he needs to heal in order to feel healthy himself.

Maybe it was because he knew me from the screen, but we felt comfortable with each other immediately. He sat with his feet under him on a sofa and smiled with the warmth of a young man who was happy with himself. He was handsome, easy with humor and sharing himself.

Over tea and crackers he told me about himself and his background.

Gasparetto was born into a middle-class family on August 16, 1949, in São Paulo, Brazil. His parents were spiritual mediums, which is not unusual in Brazil. His mother, Dona Zibia Gasparetto, herself a famous medium, was raised a Catholic, but was influenced by her spiritualist husband to abandon formal religion and study the interpretations of the Christian Gospels published by the French medium Allen Kardec.

Kardec spiritualism is very popular in Brazil, where many centers operate in his name. So Luis had a childhood of encouragement to develop his early mediumistic talents—which were naturally recognized by his mother and father.

He began to channel painters when he was thirteen. No one quite realized what was happening because the paintings were not signed, his people were not familiar with the works of the great European artists, and Gasparetto himself had very little talent for painting when *not* in trance.

He was eventually "discovered" by a visiting journalist who recognized the various styles of the paintings and pointed out that Luis was channeling the great artists.

As the years went on, his mediumship became acute and sensitive and the paintings magnificent, which led him into a period of self-deception where he believed *he* was doing the painting. Within a few weeks the painters deserted him and he was producing nothing that resembled art. He accepted this as proof that he was genuinely channeling spiritual art, and acknowledged his egotistical regression, but he found that it took a year for the painters to return. When all was intact again, he committed his life to acting as a medium and a teacher of what he learns and experiences, in order to demonstrate that death is nothing to be afraid of, and the artists prove that art, as life, is eternal and timeless.

After our tea and chat Luis led me into the dining room.

He put on a pair of overalls with acrylic paint splashed all over them. Then he brought out a bag of acrylics. He dumped these on the dining-room table and with a flourish turned on the tape recorder set to a very high volume, playing some kind of Brazilian waltz music. He then leaned over the table and seemed to go into an altered state of some kind. It didn't take very long, about one minute. Then Maria put an empty canvas flat on the table in front of him. As though he were in a film that had been speeded up, Luis *became* another energy and with great speed began to squirt acrylic paint all over the canvas. He made guttural sounds and then began to knead and push the paint around with almost insane force and speed. His right and left hands were "painting" simultaneously! Then he spoke English with a Dutch accent.

I wondered why he wasn't speaking Dutch. But I had long since learned that "entities" speaking through mediums use the knowledge and comfortable "information bank" of the medium because it does not tax the medium's energies as much as forcing through a foreign language. I have observed mediums channeling entities who spoke in languages completely foreign to the medium. In those cases, however, the mediums were exhausted afterward.

Now Luis was talking about how painting had helped him deal with his insanity! He seemed to have become van Gogh in front of my eyes. He then proceeded to paint a still life of flowers in a vase in about three minutes! It was so fast and furious I felt involved in a time warp. The painting was not like van Gogh's *Sunflowers,* which it echoed only in that it was a vase of flowers. But the broad, heavy strokes, the furious energy, the baldly stated composition were all there, and all clearly in the style of van Gogh! Luis had said his artists never repeated any painting they had done in the past. They are still progressing on the other side even though they need to paint in their old style in this world in order to be recognized.

Luis used no brushes. His fingers applied various degrees of pressure, effecting lines and curves and shapes according to the force that guided them. He used the heel of his hand, his knuckles, and so on. It was as though an invisible guidance "understood" how an effect could be achieved that bore no resemblance to traditional techniques of art.

As soon as the van Gogh canvas was complete, Luis cast it aside on the carpet. Another canvas was quickly placed in front of him. The energy coming from Luis changed. It felt more abrupt, more demanding and crisp. Luis began to speak English with a Spanish accent different from his own Portuguese. His arms and hands began to move with more precision as he forcefully grabbed more tubes of acrylic and squirted the colors onto the fresh canvas. In a moment Picasso began to talk about the need for discipline and work! The voice was gruff and much deeper in tone than Luis's. He painted what looked like the side of a face with violent green and red colors. It was masculine and sparse. The eye was lopsided, of course. Completing this subject also took about three minutes. Luis then brushed that canvas to the floor. Again his energy shifted. It was a remarkable display of prolific personality alteration. All the time the music continued to play, loud and harsh, almost as though the painters were absorbing the vibration of the sound and using it to carry their movements.

Suddenly Luis became more languid and soft. A smile drifted across his face. (From the beginning his eyes had been closed and he shielded them from whatever light was reflected in the room. He preferred to paint in darkness.)

The soft smile continued. He was painting the face of a young girl, gently and with adoration. I felt tears well up in my eyes and stream down my face. I didn't know why I was crying. Now Luis began to speak in French. It wasn't Luis, though. As the painting of the young girl evolved, I realized that the artist must be Renoir. He said something to me about my emotion in French. I easily answered him in French—though I speak very little French, somehow I found myself speaking with him quite fluently.

He spoke of her face and her innocence. I asked him why I was so moved. He answered that I identified with her purity. I wanted to ask if somehow I knew her or recognized her, but I didn't. He said he understood what I was thinking, but he didn't answer the question in my mind.

Luis lovingly patted and prodded the nuances of her delicate face with his fingertips and knuckles. All the while I cried. Gently he pushed the canvas to the floor and waited.

Luis then began to laugh mischievously. He was suddenly lighthearted and fatherly.

On the bottom of a fresh canvas he squirted purples and blues, then orange and reds on top. I saw that he had outlined a face. He turned to me with his eyes closed and spoke English with a French accent.

" 'Allo," said a voice that was distinctly not that of Luis.

I felt something familiar immediately. I wiped the tears from my eyes and answered him.

"Hello," I said.

"It is nice to see you again," he went on. He painted as he spoke.

"Oh?" I answered. "How did you know me?"

"Know you?" he chided. "I took you in. You were often one of my models."

"I was?"

"Yes."

"Where?"

"Pigalle," he answered.

My mind flashed. Pigalle? I remembered how comfortable I had felt shooting two films in the Pigalle section of Paris—*Irma La Douce* and *Can Can*.

"You have been in Pigalle many times," he went on, "as your films indicate."

"Who are you?" I asked.

He laughed. "I am your guardian and friend," he said. "I am Toulouse."

"Toulouse-Lautrec?" I felt simultaneously silly and exhilarated.

"But of course," he answered. "I am painting you in your lifetime with me in Pigalle."

I looked at the developing face. She was rather chinless with decidedly homely features.

"You were not beautiful," he said. "But you enjoyed the men and they enjoyed you."

I laughed. "Was I a hooker?"

He didn't laugh. "No," he said. "You were a dancer

from the Netherlands who had difficulty finding work there. Therefore, you migrated to Paris. You made your living many ways. One of them being a model for me. We were good friends."

I watched him finish the portrait. She had orange-red hair. He was right about the face.

"You were obsessed then, as you are now, with a concern about fatness. You must realize, my child, that holding on to fat is holding on to the past. Let the fat be part of the past. Allow it to go. Enjoy the present where there is no fat."

I had been thinking about losing weight all morning. In fact, all the way to Orange County I had been calculating what it would take to drop ten pounds or two inches. I stared at the medium who was channeling an energy who knew my private thoughts and was painting me in a lifetime I had always suspected I had had. He smiled and finished.

"Your name was Janette," he said as he titled the painting and deftly signed his initials. Then he spoke deliberately in a pronouncement.

"We artists are together in our nonphysical dimension to prove that we never passed out of existence, we only passed the earth plane."

"I see," I said. "What do you see when you paint like this?"

"We see light," he answered. "Every color has a light vibration. We feel the vibration through the hands of the instrument. We enjoy it."

His painting of Janette completed and his statement of purpose expressed, I had the feeling he needed to depart to allow more artists to come through. He didn't present me with the painting of myself. It was all too matter-of-fact for that. Instead, the canvas was brushed to the floor like the others, as Luis proceeded with more artists, more speed, and more incredible feats.

His rhythm speeded up. His head rocked back and forth. His eyes remained tightly closed and his left hand was now covering his face. He changed the tape in the recorder as if by rote to a loud classical Brazilian piece. He proceeded to channel Modigliani, Monet, Manet, Leonardo da Vinci, and a Brazilian painter called Partinari. He changed from acrylics to crayons, to watercolors, to oils depending on the needs of the artist. When he wished to clean his palms, he simply brushed them down the front of his overalls. He never opened his eyes and never took more than fifteen minutes on any subject. Most required a much shorter period of time. Sometimes the physical act of painting occurred with such force that we needed to hold on to the canvas so he wouldn't paint it off the table. He sometimes rested his head on his left arm while the right arm continued to be directed by the unseen artist.

Then he took oils with his left hand, rested his right hand, and began to paint with his left hand. I looked closely. The painting was just as well done. At the same time he began painting again with his right hand. He was painting two different pictures on two separate canvases with two separate hands! I looked at the picture painted by the left hand. It was Modigliani and he was painting it upside down!

This session went on for about an hour—painting after painting—all great artists, one after another, as though they had waited in line in some heavenly garret to come through once more and express themselves on Earth. Each signed his own painting and quickly departed to make room for the next.

Finally Luis dropped a blank canvas to the floor. He removed his shoes and socks (still in the altered state of consciousness), turned up the legs of his overalls, chose some tubes of colors, opened them, and dropped them onto the canvas on the floor. With his toes he squeezed the tubes of color into the outlines he desired and began to paint with his feet! At the same time he placed two more canvases on the table and simultaneously, with Rembrandt painting with his feet, Monet and Picasso painted respectively with the left and right hands. It was absolutely unbelievable.

In twelve minutes there were three more paintings, each artist signing his work at the same time!

I was exhausted.

Luis came out of trance. He opened his eyes, blinked at the afternoon light, and smiled. He looked down at the canvases casually.

"Choose what you like," he said.

I told him about Toulouse painting me as Janette.

"You must have it," said Luis. "Take several."

I chose the first van Gogh, the Renoir because I was so moved, Toulouse's Janette for obvious reasons, and the one-eyed Picasso for Anne Marie, who was going in for an eye operation the next day.

As Luis and I chatted for another hour he explained what he felt like before actually painting.

"I feel changes take place in my muscles and nerves," he said. "As though the artists are preparing my body. Then I feel as though something wonderful is about to happen. I am covered with a layer of sweet energy. They then speak to me telepathically and tell me what they are going to do. When I go into trance, I hear them tell me I am ready to begin. From then on the sensation is different as they take control of my body. I can feel each painter has a different vibration and personality. Some are more friendly than others. I feel van Gogh's tortured soul. It is difficult. Picasso is impatient and gruff, and becomes upset when people talk as he works. He is so temperamental sometimes he stops and tears the canvas. Toulouse is my most constant companion. He likes to discuss his work with me. Once he was concerned over his expertise in anatomy. He used a session, at which there were many people observing, to practice. He sketched many, many nudes in different poses. My mother lifted the canvases and saw what he had done and was shocked. She apologized to everyone. Toulouse disappeared for three months. When he returned I asked where he had been. He said he was told to go away and meditate on the responsibility artists have for how pictures impress the minds of people."

Luis went on to tell me of the different relationships he had with the various artists. His body could tolerate them all, and since being made aware of what it was he was doing, he had learned that he had made an agreement with them to serve as their medium before he ever came into this life. He said he did it because he knew the end of this century would be a time when it was crucial for people to understand that communication between the "dead" and the living must exist, and that the spirit of mankind evolves and develops but remains eternal.

We talked together until I realized I needed to beat the traffic on the freeway back to Los Angeles.

That day with Luis Gasparetto was one of such sweet pleasure that he brings a smile to my face when I think of him. I don't understand this phenomenon, yet it's very simple to allow myself to accept it. I remember so many moments of artistic inspiration in my own life when I was convinced that what was happening wasn't coming from me. Who was it? In the truest sense of the word, perhaps all of it is God *impersonating* people!

14

Light from Within

What we are and what we may be
Is revealed by the light within.

Mauricio Panisset was born March 6, 1930, in Minas Gerais, Brazil. He was the third child born into a family in which the father, a Methodist minister, was also interested in metaphysics. But shortly Mauricio's mother claimed she couldn't handle her son's uncontrollable rebelliousness. Out of desperation, when he was nine years old, his parents sent him to live with his grandmother on a farm, where it was hoped the greater freedom would give some release to his bounding spirit.

He often walked to the forest where he (later) claimed that "lights" followed him. The lights appeared as shimmering balls and "talked" to him whenever they appeared. But out of fear that he would be even more unacceptable to his family and to his new home, at the time he told no one of his encounters.

When he reached puberty the lights disappeared.

In 1949, at age nineteen, he joined the army and

one night while he was on watch the lights reappeared. Now he nurtured and developed his loving relationship with them and read fervently the works of Blavatsky, Leadbetter, and Alice Bailey, the Kabala, and whatever other esoteric literature he could find. He also plunged deeply into the study of Buddhism, Shiism, and Hinduism.

In 1953, out of the army, he became a 33 degree Mason (advanced student of metaphysics).

He married, fathered several children, divorced, and married again. In 1966, he was employed by the Department of the Minister of Education. While working on their broadcasting tower, he fell one hundred and twenty feet. He thought he was going to die, but instead he only fractured his leg and never even lost consciousness. He regarded the event as a miracle and determined for himself that his survival had something to do with the lights and therefore concluded that he must have a "mission."

After the fall from the tower the lights never left him. Moreover, they seemed different. In their presence he was more psychically aware and found he could access the Akashic Records (events, said to be stored in ether energy, that can be tapped by someone who is sensitive) and know the past lives of people.

In 1969 the lights became so strong that they again began to "speak."

On April 19, 1969, one of the lights spoke so strongly that Mauricio could not ignore it. It said,

"You must use your own light to heal the sick. You must go to the hospital and begin." Mauricio became ill, irritated, and disoriented. He was unable to sleep. The doctors told him he was just nervous and tired. Mauricio felt he was going crazy. He did not, as the lights continued to command, set out to heal people. He did not believe he had the power and was totally involved in raising his large family and making his second marriage work. His health did not improve.

Then late one night he was driving on the road with his wife and four children. The lights followed alongside the car. Mauricio stopped the car and got out. He felt a strong heat on the right side of his spine. One very prominent blue light came toward him. It stopped and in front of him it materialized into a transparent being who called himself Uhr. He told Mauricio it was necessary for him to heal the sick for his *own* health. Mauricio looked over at his wife and children in the car and asked them if they were seeing what he was seeing. They nodded. Uhr departed.

Still, it was two years before Mauricio responded to this roadside encounter. He really did not *want* to be a healer. But as soon as he complied, his own health improved.

Several years later another experience occurred. Again Mauricio was driving. Again he was followed by lights. Again he stopped, whereupon a bright yellow light approached him and materialized into a being who called himself Akron.

"You must continue to heal," said Akron. "That is your agreement."

By now the beings of light had become common-place for Mauricio, but for others it was astonishing. As he healed with the energy from his hands, the lights began to appear during the healing process. And soon after that the first signs of chakra stigmata began to appear on his chest. The chakra stigmata were scar shapes that appeared to have been burned into his skin. The first to appear was a small cross on the skin of his chest. It never appeared raw; it looked as though it had been healed for some time.

In 1980 Mauricio was outside enjoying the sunset at his ranch in Fazenda das Parteiras as the evening drew in. A heavy rain cloud appeared and opened up. Out of the center of the cloud three starlike lights appeared and came toward him. As they approached they didn't get bigger. When he directed his flashlight on them, they disappeared. The three lights then merged into one large ball of light. Mauricio felt a message in his head. "I am Enoch," it said. "Go more to the hospitals to heal. Time is short. I will be with you."

Mauricio objected. "I haven't any more time," he said. "I don't care if time is short, I have my own problems."

Enoch said, "There will be no more problems for you."

Mauricio felt a hot sensation on his chest as the light of Enoch hovered for forty minutes. Then it was gone.

When Mauricio undressed for bed that night he saw that there were new scars of chakra stigmata burned into the skin at each of the seven chakra centers on his body. And on his chest was burned the star of Enoch. After that the lights were with him constantly. Whenever Mauricio played hooky from healing, the Enoch light would appear to scold and urge him to continue healing others and demand explanations as to why he was not working at it.

Today Mauricio Panisset is a healer unlike any other.

Again, it was Anne Marie Bennstrom who brought him to my attention. She flew him from Brazil, where she had met him in the course of her metaphysical-spiritual searchings, and subsequently she brought him to my house on Mount Rainier. The mountain had never seen such a light show.

When Mauricio walked into my home I felt as if I were meeting a cross between Charlie Chaplin and Cantinflas (the Mexican comic genius I had worked with in *Around the World in 80 Days*). Mauricio embraced me warmly and I was aware that he had a beer belly (which turned out to be a wine belly). His trousers were clutched up by a belt and he walked with a kind of comic shuffle.

He wore a shirt open at the collar and when he leaned over I could see the chakra burns and the star of Enoch on his chest. He was flanked by two women, named Maria and Francesca, along with Anne Marie. He was about five-foot-four, stout, white-haired, and tanned naturally by the sun. He was obviously used to being the center of attention and also clearly would have had no problem heading up his own harem.

His eyes twinkled with mischief, yet I felt there was a deep wisdom in this man despite his apparent need to play the holy fool. He began to make jokes in his broken English immediately, and in an almost seductive manner.

My assistant, Simo, and I served everyone wine and snacks and we chatted about Mauricio's life and healing until the sun went down.

Mauricio told me that there were two light beings who were with him constantly—Akron and Shalla. "They protect me with light. They help me heal. You will see."

Well, "see" I did.

I have seen quite a bit of psychic phenomena, some of it impressive, some not. This was phenomenal.

I think Mauricio needed the wine to relax, although as we spoke about it, he claimed he didn't. In any case, one bottle (for himself) later, he felt ready to begin.

From a comfortable sitting position on my couch, Mauricio suddenly jumped up. As he did, a flash of light occurred in the living room. It had no traceable source. It just flashed. I wondered if someone was taking flashbulb pictures, although this light was much brighter.

Mauricio then grabbed me by the hand and said, "Come."

He took me to the guest room where he would sleep. There was a stereo tape deck in the room, which he immediately turned on. A tape of deep, resonant chanting had been racked up.

"Lie on bed, please," he commanded. Anne Marie and the others remained in the living room. I had no idea what would happen to me.

I lay on the bed. Mauricio seemed to be checking the direction of my head. "You turn around," he said. "Head to the electromagnetic north." I turned around. I lay there quietly waiting. I could make him out in the dark. He just stood across the room, quite still, as though waiting for instruction.

Then suddenly Mauricio moved over and fell to his knees beside the bed, bowed his head, and began to chant and pray. He drew in deep, deep breaths, breathing in a manner I had never seen. He spent a long time breathing in concentration. The Oming, chanting music continued.

Mauricio raised his body from his prayer position. He breathed in again deeply and then with all his concentration he breathed out with a *pow!* sound. The entire room lit up with light coming from the solar plexus of his body. I saw a jagged electrical charge emanate from the center of his torso and flash down his arms, through his hands, and out into the room! George Lucas would have been hard pressed to duplicate such an effect. I was astonished, startled, and completely thrown by the intensity of the electrical light that had come from his body. Then I heard a sizzling sound followed by the smell of ozone in the air. Was this for real? Just as I questioned what I saw, he stood up. I could see hir.. move in the stillness of the dark room. He stood behind my head by the bed. He leaned over me and began to "read" the energy in my body by holding his hands flat, palms down, over my body. Then he touched each of my seven energy centers and "read" the chakras as he went. As he did this he continued to breathe deeply and in a state of "mentalization," as he described it later.

He leaned down to my face and placed his forehead on my forehead (his third eye on my third eye). He breathed deeply again, and then, as though getting a signal from the unseen guide, he let out a great gust of air by making that *pow* sound, whereupon an electrical charge of light came jagging through his forehead into mine. It was a shock to me because I was not prepared. But it did not hurt. I assumed he was opening up my third eye center, from which much psychic awareness flows. Immediately it felt as though sparks of gentle electricity fell into my eyes. My eyeballs tingled. My scalp felt singed. I wondered if I would have burn scars like his on my forehead. My mind flashed to how I would look in a close-up! Then I thought I could always play parts with bangs.

Mauricio didn't stop with just one jolt of electrical light through my forehead. He did it three times. I laughed to myself. It must have been one for mind, one for body, and one for spirit.

The third-eye charge completed, he came around to the side of the bed and placed his hands on my heart chakra. He pressed down, breathed in again, and like a heart doctor attempting to pump a heart into beating again, he pumped and *powed* simultaneously as a great ball of jagged electricity fused through his hands into my body where I assumed my heart was.

I felt myself stand back as an observer.

It would be hard to prove I wasn't dreaming.

Mauricio "electrified" my heart several times and each time the electromagnetic shapes of the light were different.

He stepped away from the bed and began to flick his hands in midair as though to recharge his batteries. The deep breathing continued. He breathed out and his body lit up in jagged electrical charges of light. As he worked, the entire room lit up. I was to learn later that the light he emitted in the bedroom flashed through the walls of the house, illuminating every other room too! (I have since seen him do all of this in broad daylight wearing only a G-string to prove there was no concealment of any kind of mechanical light device.)

Then Mauricio knelt on one knee and placed his body in different positions. Since the room was dark

I could only make out his silhouette when he charged the room with the electrical energy. Then the image would be etched on my eyes much as it would be in a storm of lightning at night. Next, he assumed a position with his arm above his head. His body appeared to become a lightning rod, a current of light streaking from the center of his being out through the tips of his fingers.

At the completion of this dazzling light display Mauricio lurched out of the room and fell to the floor in the hallway, exhausted. I got up from the bed and went to him. He was perspiring profusely and badly needed water. As I tended to him in the hallway, the lights continued to spark and flash from the bedroom! It was science fiction fantasy—but it was actually occurring.

Anne Marie brought him water. He drank several glasses one after another, continuing to emit light flashes as he drank. He got up suddenly and went into the bathroom, leaving the door open. He unzipped his trousers, and as he urinated into the toilet bowl the stream of urine itself was light!

Anne Marie laughed. "Have you ever seen anything like this?" she asked.

"No," I answered, in shock. In fact, I wondered if I really *was* seeing it.

When Mauricio came out of the bathroom, he was out of his altered state. We all went into the living room. He wanted wine. I wondered if the wine would light up. It didn't. He drank it before it had a chance.

Presently, possibly strengthened by the wine, Mauricio proceeded to display his illuminating light healing techniques for Simo and me again, and this went on for hours. In between glasses of wine he went out on the balcony and lit up the landscaped gardens around my house as though it were daylight.

I was watching so carefully for objects capable of such illumination. He held nothing in his hands.

It would have been impossible to produce such dazzling light from a mechanical object anyway, because the light emanated from *inside* his body. I saw the source of it. It was as though there was an internal lightning rod charging his physical form. Flashes of light appeared in every room. Were his entities Akron and Shalla enjoying their own party? It was all beyond me. It was like being in another dimension of reality. Was he the conduit for bringing physical and light dimensions together? Were we healed just by being in his presence? He didn't seem terribly spiritual or even particularly reverent to what he was doing. He took it as a matter of course.

"I balance the chakras with light force," he would say casually. "It is Enoch. It is Akron and Shalla. It is God. It is *not* me."

He would then have more wine and make more jokes.

"Show them your chakras," Anne Marie commanded Mauricio. With a glass of wine in one hand, he opened his shirt and displayed the stigmata on each of his chakras as he drank. In perfectly aligned positions physically indicating the location of the esoteric chakras within, there were circular burns. They glowed and pulsed.

"Sometimes they bleed if he doesn't heal," Anne Marie said. Mauricio nodded and smiled and sipped wine until he got the urge to light up again. I assumed that the "urge" was directed from Akron and Shalla, who were monitoring the energies of those of us who needed more balancing and healing.

When I offered Mauricio food for dinner he refused. He continued to joke, sip wine, and play with his lights. He walked around *powing* and teasing, tweaking us ladies under the chin, and singing children's nursery rhymes.

As I observed him I reflected on how solemn we expect metaphysicality to be. When someone has the capacity to bridge dimensions, somehow we expect to genuflect and speak with hushed reverence. Mauricio expected nothing of the kind; in fact, he scoffed at the suggestion and preferred an attitude of comic tomfoolery. Perhaps this aspect of his character accounted for his original long reluctance to act as a healing channel.

At about 2:00 A.M., Mauricio suggested we all sleep for the night. He would be up for a while longer, but the rest of us should rest.

"I want to do a light healing before you sleep," he said.

I led him into my bedroom, crawled into bed with my clothes on, and he stood over me.

"Protection for her," he said to his guides of light. Whereupon he went into a series of brilliant illuminative flashes that made what had occurred earlier in the evening look like dark victory. My entire bedroom and the balcony outside lit up. I could see Mount Rainier etched in light outside the window. The light flashes emanating from him were constant now, with no pauses in between. It was awesome, incredible, beyond reason. Yet I felt myself becoming more and more peaceful, and when at last he went and I fell asleep, I slept more gently than I ever had in my life.

The next day Mauricio left, and as I was walking by the river I noticed how much more appreciation I seemed to have for everything around me that was alive. I felt areas of compassion that I had never touched before. I wanted to cry out of love for anyone in trouble or hurting. I wanted to do more to help people. I sat down on an old log and tried to meditate. Instead, I found myself quietly sobbing because as I looked at the wilderness around me I realized that love was what held everything together. I didn't know where that love came from, but I knew it was in me and everything around me. It was one of those windows in time when I felt I was finally understanding.

I sat on the log marveling at the role "light" seemed to have played in an *emotional* experience. What was the connection? Was light the physical extension of love? Was light the manner in which we translated the God energy into reality?

I remembered all the people who, during their out-of-body experiences, saw the brilliant white light and said they "knew" it was God. Always accompanying that light was an overwhelming feeling of love. Therefore, if we find light do we find love? Was light the vibration of love that we could tolerate? Was there an even more brilliant light waiting for us in the vast dominion of cosmic understanding?

Perhaps this was how science and spirituality would meet. In the struggle of science to explain God and creation, perhaps the answer lay in the subatomic light particles that seemed to be dancing as a kind of glue, holding consciousness together. Were these subatomic light particles really particles of God energy? Could it be conceptually that simple? And in being that simple did we humans find it unacceptable because we preferred not to take the responsibility for understanding?

Some months later, I invited Mauricio to come from Brazil to perform and heal at a four-day seminar I was conducting on Memorial Day weekend in California. He said he had "lost his lights," because he hadn't been living up to his "destiny's responsibility" to heal. I proposed that this would be an opportunity for him to correct his neglect. He agreed and made the trip.

As soon as he entered the room, where three hundred people waited for the surprise I had promised, he said he felt his "light friends" return. He gazed out at the small crowd and immediately proceeded to reorganize where they sat. "I've never healed in a group so large," he said to me quietly. "Their energy patterns need to be dispersed, else my own circuits will be overloaded." He rearranged them into three groups and asked them not to send him energy of any kind. He had enough of his own!

Standing quietly before the group, he began to breathe deeply, meditate, breathe again, and finally, with his familiar *pow* outtake of air, he turned himself into a human lightning rod.

I got a kick out of the crowd's reaction, remembering my own. They were astonished, incredulous, delighted, some of them suspicious, and yet each of them seemed to realize that something was actually occurring that was beyond our present acceptance and assessment of logical reality. His light display went on for about an hour. Some people claimed they were cured of various aches and pains; others sobbed at the release of what they had done to their own bodies and felt clear of that self-tension. Still others simply basked in the flashes of light, not knowing, understanding, or even caring about a logical explanation. If they *perceived* this to be a healing process it would be.

In short, the evening was a success, not only for the group, but for Mauricio and the return of his light friends.

The following morning, as people were leaving and making travel plans by phone, I heard two New York lawyers, who had been present at Mauricio's performance, talking to fellow members of their law firm, in New York. They described what had happened the night before. There was a silence. Then one of them said, "But I saw it with my own eyes." The other one said, "But he never touched his body to push an electrical switch or anything." More silence. I could imagine the incredulity on the other end of the phone; subtle accusations of hallucination or something similar. Soon the two lawyers hung up. They looked at each other, blushed back their embarrassment, and almost simultaneously said, "They didn't believe me. They said I couldn't have seen it."

I stepped over to them. I put my hands on their shoulders, trying not to appear too patronizing. "Welcome to the club," I said. "You'll get used to it. And so will the ones who called you crazy."

15

My Body as Ultimate Atoms of Awareness

*Where there is no resistance
there is no harm.*

I finally tried something that I had heard about for years. Because it involved my own physical body and because I actually experienced it as a legitimate event seemingly without fraud, it was the single most impactful incident in my attempt to understand the link between the physical and nonphysical worlds.

I will simply relate what happened.

I had seen many videotapes of psychic surgery operations brought back from Brazil and the Philippines. One had been given to me by a medical doctor who had personally undergone treatment and was cured of an eye disease. I had read many books about the lives of the psychic surgeons and had talked to others who claimed to have been healed by them.

I had also seen "magicians" on evening talk shows attempt to debunk the phenomenon with very well done "psychic surgery" magic acts of their own. They used chicken gizzards and red-colored pellets to simulate blood. It was usually a kind of gory sleight-of-hand act without the elegance of, say, Siegfried & Roy. I watched the debunkers with impassive curiosity. They impressed me as individuals who were exploiting what they claimed to be the naïveté and insistence of "dumb people who want to believe in the tooth fairy." Their fear and emotional violence interested me. Their "debunking of charlatans" seemed to suggest that they made their livings at it.

The videotapes that I saw were very different from the magicians' performances because the surgery had been performed in clinics with other doctors and nurses present. The patients paid no money for the healing unless they offered to pay, and the emotional ambience of the environment was peaceful and indeed prayerful.

Still, I had made enough movies with remarkable special effects to doubt what I was seeing on tape. I needed to see it in person. And I wanted to keep an open mind.

In one particularly impressive film, however, I watched the Reverend Alex Orbito from Manila operate, one after another, on a long queue of people. He gently kneaded the skin of each patient until it opened up. He then inserted his hands into the body wherever there was sickness, withdrew clots of blood and internal matter of some kind, and withdrew his hands, whereupon the "incision" closed up. There was blood

on the patient but hardly a trace of a scar. The
camera ran continuously—that is, without any cuts.
He operated on about twenty people in twenty minutes. Each operation took approximately sixty seconds, and there were ailments of every description
from ulcers to back pain, to goiter, cancer, brain
tumors, eye diseases, and heart problems. The tape
was remarkable, but I didn't trust it.

A friend of mine told me that Alex Orbito was in
America. I told my daughter, Sachi, who had been
having back and neck pain. It was Sachi who first
had the courage to go to Alex, and when she described the procedure, I decided it was important
that I meet him.

It was funny to me that his next healing stop was
Las Vegas, the scene of so many physically and spiritually powerful engagements for me.

Immediately after Sachi's healing with Alex, her
pain disappeared. But he warned her that if the pain
stemmed from a karmic cause she would have to
work that out herself by aligning herself with the
God energy more faithfully than she had up till then.

I called Chris Griscom, the spiritual acupuncturist
from Galisteo, and asked her to meet me in Vegas.
We took a hotel room right off the Strip and waited
to see the Reverend Alex Orbito, who was famous
not only in the Philippines but all over the world.

Orbito was born on November 25, 1940, in one of
the barrios of Cuyapo, Nueva Ecija, a province in the
Philippines, about two hundred kilometers north-

west of Manila. His parents were poor. They tilled land belonging to their landlord.

Orbito was not aware of his healing power until he was fourteen, when he began to have dreams about a mysterious old man who said he was the boy's spirit guide and gave him a personal mantra that enabled Alex to place himself in an altered state of consciousness at will. In these dreams the old man told Alex he was a great healer.

Alex paid no attention until one morning the paralyzed mother of a friend of his called, claiming that she had had a dream the night before that Alex had cured her of her paralysis. Immediately Alex realized he had had the same dream!

He went to the old woman. They recognized each other, though they had never met. Without a word he picked up a bottle of coconut oil beside her bed, massaged her legs as he had in his dream, said a deep but short prayer, and commanded her to walk.

Immediately she rose from her bed for the first time in ten years and walked.

From then on he realized he *was* a healer, possessing in his hands an energy he didn't understand.

He didn't want to be a healer, however. What he didn't understand was frightening to him. Moreover, after the fame of his talent spread, people exploited his gift, many times sending for him, paying him nothing, and leaving him to return to his village by his own devices.

Eventually he became a reverend of the Union

Espiritista Christiana de Felipinas and stopped healing. Immediately he became ill. He went back to
healing—his health was fine again. He noticed that
whenever he quit healing people in need, *he* became
sick. From then on he decided to devote his life to
serving humanity through spiritual healing. He traveled throughout the Philippines, healing hundreds of
people for practically nothing, and at last established
a clinic of his own near his modest house in Quezon
City.

Chris and I chatted before Orbito arrived. She had
heard of him and said it would be an honor to have
him work on her. I wasn't so sure.

I opened the hotel room door and there stood a
very young-looking, extremely thin man, impeccably
dressed in an immaculate white shirt, tie, slacks, and
a satin football jacket. He was with his wife and a
woman friend of hers. The smile on his face put me
at ease immediately. From the moment we all met I
felt I had always known him.

Knowing and liking him was one thing. Having
him perform "spiritual surgery" was another.

After some socializing in the living room we re-
tired to the bedroom of my hotel suite. Alex looked
at the bed and I knew that was where it would all
happen.

His wife and her friend took an empty plastic bowl

from a fresh paper bag, along with some gauze and alcohol. My stomach clutched.

Alex sat on a chair near the bed.

"I do not heal," he said quietly. "God heals. He uses me only as an instrument and channeler for the healing force and energy. I balance the chakras so an individual can heal himself." Again I was reminded of how important the chakras seemed to be.

Chris smiled. I wondered what would happen.

First of all, there was really nothing wrong with me. I was not sick. Nothing was bothering me. So I suddenly wondered why I was there, and why I had asked him to come! As soon as I wondered that, I felt something within me (my Higher Self?) say, "Because you need to trust the physical experience of a higher vibration."

Fine, but I wasn't about to go first. I gestured to Chris. She lay on the bed.

Alex bowed his head and went into a deep, silent prayer for about five minutes. When he lifted his face there was an intense yet beatific expression upon it. He had told us that another spiritual doctor worked through him and his energy would perform the surgery.

"Take off blouse," Alex said. "I must work on heart." Chris lifted her blouse off over her head. I was glad she was wearing a bra. I remembered I wasn't.

Alex's wife and assistant sat beside him.

As though by command Alex's arms went up in

the air, found a direction of some kind, then gently plunged downward into Chris's midsection, whereupon he deftly began to knead the skin of her torso above the waist, just as I had seen on the tape, until his hands seemed to separate the skin and suddenly both hands were *inside* her chest. I couldn't believe what I was seeing. There was blood, and there was a sloshing sound as his hands searched around for something near her heart.

I looked closely at Chris. She groaned with pleasure, saying, "The heat of his hands, I feel this fabulous healing heat."

To me it appeared his hands were actually inside her chest! Very gently, with his right hand he removed something that looked like a clot of blood. He placed it in the plastic bowl. His left hand remained in her chest.

Then, as though he had gotten directions from his healing source, he said, "Now your kidneys." He removed his hands from Chris's chest and the opening closed up as though he had simply withdrawn his hands from a dish of water. His wife wiped off the blood with gauze soaked in alcohol.

Immediately, his hands plunged into Chris's abdomen. Again she remarked about the heat. This time his hands were wrist-deep in her abdomen. Blood and liquids were sloshing everywhere as he seemed to gently rock his hands back and forth inside of her! I went to the edge of the bed and looked down.

I gasped. I couldn't help myself. His hands were

literally inside her abdomen up to his wrists! I slapped my own face to ensure I wasn't dreaming. Then I began to pace around the room. I felt I was in some other kind of reality. I came close and leaned over Chris's stomach again. His hands were actually *in* there! Both of them. And no, I wasn't dreaming.

"What does it feel like?" I asked Chris.

"Well," she said with a slight frown, "I feel it, but it's more like a pressure feeling. There is no pain."

Alex was oblivious to our conversation. It was as though he was *somewhere* and *someone* else.

Very quickly he removed more clots of blood from her abdomen, put them in the plastic bowl, and withdrew his hands. I watched carefully. Again it was as though his hands had been in water instead of a human body. It was so smooth, so unbelievably simple and easy. The deep, gaping opening closed. Again his wife washed away the blood with an alcohol-soaked gauze, and Chris simply got up from the bed. She was smiling. She was obviously fine.

"Please," Alex said, gesturing to me.

"Oh God," I thought. "I'm a dancer, a physical culturist. I like to be in control of my own body. I don't like regular surgery, much less this kind."

Reluctantly I lay on the bed.

"Pancreas," Alex said immediately, as though he had been directed from some unknown source. His hands were poised above my chest. I looked over at Chris, then at him.

"Wait a minute," I said, feeling like a chicken-hearted jerk. I couldn't go through with it. Chris smiled and sat down on the bed. Then I reached for Alex's wife's hand. I needed reassurance.

Alex simply waited. Only it didn't seem to be Alex.

I closed my eyes. I tried to meditate and make contact with my Higher Self. I couldn't find it. I was too nervous. I was beside myself. I had arranged all of this and now I wished I hadn't. Did nervousness mean it could hurt me because I didn't have enough trust and faith? "Oh God," I thought, "what the hell am I doing here?"

I closed my eyes again. Silently I pleaded, "Higher Self, come in, please. Come in please, Higher Self. I need to communicate." I felt like Spock tuning in to the *Enterprise*.

I waited. Alex waited. Chris waited. The wife and friend-assistant waited.

Then slowly, with my eyes closed, I went within myself. I put my fear out of my mind. Slowly my Higher Self swam into view. I'll never forget it. There was my androgynous friend sitting on a rock with its chin on its knee like Rodin's *The Thinker*. Only this time my personal "being" had wings. I laughed to myself. This was truly science fiction space opera.

Yet I was so relieved and happy to make contact. Then I saw that the smile my androgynous being gave me was definitely patronizing.

"Should I do this?" I asked. I couldn't believe I asked such a question.

My Higher Self looked at me with disdain and

remarked, in a manner very unbefitting its Divine stature, "You're a real jerk, you know that? *This* experience is what you have created for yourself so you'll have proof that the body is nothing but 'dream thought.' Now relax and proceed."

I opened my eyes and looked at Alex and nodded. "Go ahead," I said. "I'm ready."

Before I got "I'm ready" out of my mouth, his hands gently descended on my pancreas area and before I knew it they were inside my body and he was removing what he called "negative energy clots." I wanted to say it was what was left of the hot fudge sundae I had had the day before, but that kind of humor didn't seem appropriate. I couldn't bring myself to look down at the hands inside me. I kept my eyes closed.

"How does it look?" I asked Chris.

"It's incredible," she said. "I can see inside you. What do you feel?"

I wanted to say something funny but I found myself saying, "I feel like it's a reality dream."

"Sure," Chris answered. "That's what the physical body is—a dream that we have dreamed into believing is real so we can have the adventure of physical life."

I wasn't really in shape for that kind of metaphysical dialogue. Chris smiled.

Alex withdrew his hands from my pancreas area.

"Kidneys and colon," he said. And before I could resist I lowered my slacks and his hands were gently

kneading the skin just below my navel. In about
three seconds both his hands were inside my abdomen up to the wrists. This time I looked. It was just
as it had been with Chris. I felt no pain—only pressure. There was a great deal of sloshing as blood and
guts were rocked from side to side. (Words do not
aptly describe this procedure.) He extracted more
"negative stress clots" and soon withdrew first his
right hand, then his left.

Again his wife cleaned the blood from my stomach
with alcohol-soaked gauze. The friend took the plastic bowl from the bedside to the bathroom, dumped
everything into the toilet, and returned. Alex bowed
his head and seemed to come out of his trance. He
stood up. "All right?" he asked cheerfully.

I nodded. I was speechless. He walked out of the
room, as though to prepare for lunch. I got up from
the bed and went into the bathroom. I sat on the tub
and broke down and sobbed.

The rest of the day I spent alone, trying to adjust to
what had happened. I was a body-oriented person
who needed to be in touch with the mechanisms that
made it work. My years of dancing and hard work-
outs had put me in command of my physical vehicle,
yet this slender, sensitive, almost frail-looking "spiritual healer," in an altered state of consciousness, had
put his hands through my skin and, with no pain,

had extracted what he called "negative thought forms which coagulate in the blood" and put them in a plastic bowl from the drugstore. It didn't make sense.

Was this what was meant by trusting that "the hand of God" not only can heal material matter but can pass through it without producing pain, just as though the body was nothing more than materialized thought, a fanciful plaything, a vehicle for adventure—indeed only a dream for experience. I decided this was not the time to sort that out and went back to practicalities.

Chris went back to Galisteo and I sat around the deserted pool area just thinking and mulling over everything.

My dreams that night were vivid and deep. When I woke the next day I felt absolutely wonderful: light and energetic, as though I had been unburdened of something I should not have been carrying.

"We must do more," Alex had said. "I need to balance your chakra energies. Not good, too much, too soon."

When I asked him how much money he charged he told me to contribute whatever I wanted; that he was building a healing center in the Philippines that would benefit many people who could afford very little.

I decided to have some more treatments and then decide what I would contribute.

More treatments came. In fact, the following day as I lay on the hotel bed, he did spiritual surgery on my heart, third eye, ovaries, and throat. Then he asked me to turn over while he opened up the entire length of my spinal column and took out "negative vibrations" causing pain in my back. Of course I couldn't see how he opened my back, but I *could* feel the procedure internally. It wasn't painful, it was "pressurized." I could feel his hands deep inside my back, but there was no sharpness or sting of hurt.

When he had finished, I counted up what he had done: five "operations" in a time span of about three minutes.

He explained that the spiritual energy coming through his hands was as healing for people as the actual extraction of negativity. Therefore, people could benefit regardless of whether they had anything wrong.

Maybe it was my imagination, maybe not. I only know that after my few days with Alex my energy level increased considerably. I felt balanced and capable of sleeping more deeply.

After that I read all the books on Philippine spiritual healing I could find. Those written by Western doctors expressed astonishment and, in lieu of a logical explanation, skepticism. Those written by Filipinos and other Asians, particularly the series of books by Jaime T. Licauco, expressed more of an acceptance of realities beyond our comprehension. Again, the left-brained (logical) versus the right-brained (intuitive) diversity of reaction.

In my talks with Alex Orbito himself, he outlined the tests, observations, and scientific laboratory testing he had been subjected to. I have since studied the corroborations of his claims. When I asked why he felt it was necessary for the scientific world to believe what he was doing was "real," he replied, "Because they can benefit from the hand of God and healing ministry."

Orbito had been invited to Sweden in 1974 to subject himself to Scandinavian scientists who, under laboratory conditions, examined him, searched him, asked him to heal with no clothes on, measured his heartbeat, brain waves, pulse, rate of perspiration, et cetera. Through Kirlian photography, they observed the extent of his aura and the energy coming out of his hands while he healed and operated.

Orbito said he was treated like a guinea pig and would never subject himself to those traumatic experiences again, because it was difficult to heal under circumstances of such skepticism and doubt. He said, as many doctors now also say, that to become well you need to believe that you can.

As for the accusations that Filipino surgeons use blood capsules and animal innards to create what appears to be physical proof of extraction, the evidence is confusing.

When tested in a laboratory, the blood is sometimes human blood and sometimes more of a watery plasma. The healers themselves say they don't understand why. They explain only that it isn't really necessary to break the skin and produce real blood or physical extractions to effect healing. They say that the *patient* needs physical proof that he is being healed in order to become better. So they materialize and manifest blood for that purpose. They say that if a patient "sees" he was operated upon, the healing effect is more profound. So just as they "dematerialize" the epidermis in order to enter the body, they "materialize" blood and clots to effect healing. They say the body is only an illusion anyway, the *physical* being only the manifestation of one's thought. I found the issue of physical "reality" to be the central question, not whether Alex was a fraud or not.

There was no doubt in my mind that his hands had entered my body. I had felt it and seen it, not only in myself but in others as I stood over them and observed. Had I been feeling my body itself as a physical illusion? All the spiritual masters claim that such a concept is the central issue in understanding the physical dimension in our lives; that the physical is fundamentally a coagulation of molecules that are a product of our consciousness. Consciousness then translates into projected thought and thought becomes physical reality.

Over the next few weeks I invited Orbito to my home in Malibu so I could observe more, and since it was Christmastime I put out the word that Alex would do a Christmas healing and people could contribute whatever they wanted to his healing center.

Nearly one hundred came on Christmas Day and the day after. There were friends, friends of friends, curious spiritual seekers, and some who were really ill.

Alex, his wife, and his assistant stayed in the guest rooms while I turned my yoga and workout room into a clinic.

We used my massage table for people to lie on and Alex sat on a chair behind it. His wife and assistant sat beside him, and I observed many of the "operations," some of which I never thought I could stomach witnessing, but I did. And I watched closely.

People quietly meditated before they entered the room. Nearly all of them were trusting but as anxious and frightened as I had been. I understood the contradiction. I had been through it. They supported one another, and Alex led a prayer and "communal connection to God" before we began.

Among the operations I saw was one where I witnessed him take someone's eye out of the socket with his fingers, clean behind it, and replace it. The patient felt no pain; she got up and left the table smiling, saying she felt only "pressure."

He removed tumors from lungs and abdomens.

He extracted a tooth with his fingers and stopped the bleeding.

He took cysts and growths from every imaginable part of the body.

When patients had genital problems I always left the room. They told me later Alex had removed hemorrhoids, uterine fibroids, and so on. He usually went into the body *through* the outside, rarely into the vagina or the anus.

He removed breast tumors and a goiter.

He took blood clots from the neck of an eighty-six-year-old friend who had problems with hardening arteries.

He went into the gums of someone else and healed her pyorrhea.

He took a tumor out of a brain.

Sometimes people wanted to observe others. Alex never liked more than a few at a time because he said skeptical energy drained him.

In the same holiday time period he went to Ojai to heal people there. More people from Los Angeles followed him. Many of them had come at my invitation.

I remember the first day in Ojai; Alex had set up a clinic room in the vestibule of a Unity church. Thirty people wanted to see someone else operated on before they would allow any healing on their own bodies. I volunteered, since so many were there because of me.

They quietly filed into the room. I lay on a table fully clothed. Alex was behind the table with his head in his hands, bowed in prayer. He prayed for a long time. I supposed it was because of the diversity of energies in the room (psychics and sensitives tune in to everyone else's energy patterns, which sometimes has a negative impact on them).

Alex didn't raise his head. Finally, with his head still bowed, he whispered to me. "Shirley," he said hesitantly. "There is man in blue sweater against the wall who is negative, very negative. He doesn't like me or what I do. Very difficult. You can ask him to leave please?"

I turned my head from the lying position and spotted the man he was talking about. It was the friend of a journalist whom I had invited. Rather than single him out, I said, "There is evidently some-one here exuding a lot of skeptical negative energy. You know who you are. It would be better if you came back later when you felt more positive." (I was learning to be diplomatic in my old age . . . finally.)

The man in the blue sweater, along with two other people, quietly left. No one blamed them. Alex prayed again and went into a slight trance. His expression changed and the "operation" on me proceeded. I didn't watch Alex's hands dive into my abdomen. Instead, I chose to look at the faces of the people watching. They were astonished, horrified, intrigued, shocked, stunned—how to describe how people look when they observe something that defies their sense of reality? One person exclaimed, "Oh no, Shirley, be careful!" She was so genuinely worried that from the table I reassured her. Others were astonished that I could talk while Alex had both hands up to his wrists inside my abdomen, where there were the usual slurpy sloshing noises. Blood was running quite freely down the sides of my body. I felt deep pressure inside my abdomen and I had to admit this time there was slight pain. I knew it was coming from the disbelief in the room, so I closed my eyes and put my own mind into a consciousness of complete trust. The pain subsided.

It was then that I realized so clearly the importance of trust when working with spiritual healing, or anything spiritual for that matter. At the same time I flashed on the times in my life when I believed I would get well as opposed to believing the illness would last longer. I remembered regular doctors I had had. If I trusted them, I fared better. It seemed to be as much up to me as it was to the doctor. The healer and the healed working together. On reflection, my body always reacted to my expectations. Physicality follows mind.

It was psychic surgery that put me more in touch with that understanding than I had ever been.

I remembered what Alex had said: "People need proof that they are healed, so I give it to them. I don't need to enter the body." He went on, "I could do it with magnetic healing. I don't need to extract anything in order for them to be healed. But Westerners especially feel they need that kind of *physical* proof to allow themselves to be healed spiritually, so I manifest the proof."

I've thought so often of what he said. Was that how our traditional medicine worked also? Did we need something as drastic as surgery to believe that our bodies were rid of infection, even though we were perfectly capable of healing ourselves internally with our own power?

And why did we put people dealing with alternative healing realities in laboratory conditions to obtain conclusions about which science had already programmed judgment? Scientific equipment is designed to satisfy the concept that something lives up to that which science already understands. But what about expanded reality? What about possible truth that we haven't even conceived of yet?

Many people leave spiritual healing sessions *believing* they are cured because their bodies feel better. The sickness doesn't return and they know that they are cured. But because traditional medicine doesn't understand it, are those people to be told they are *not* really healed? Should they be persuaded that spiritual energy healed them only so that they could get sick again and be cured by drugs and knife surgery?

If we as human beings are made up of a collection of so-called "non-alive simple atoms" and yet see ourselves as alive and conscious, where did the change take place? When did it happen? Can one "see" consciousness? Can we measure it?

When Alex Orbito or any other healer is working with high consciousness, void of physical form, that consciousness is what the Bible would call God, and further, would describe the process as a miracle. But suppose it is simply consciousness of a high order acting as a healer through a physical person with the right vibrations such as Alex—would that *not* present grounds for the consideration of expanded and un-known reality?

We seem to insist on being limited and lonely, forever churning on the treadmill of our own identities, incorrigibly resisting the idea that we may understand more than we allow ourselves to admit, because such an admittance would force us to see ourselves in a more expanded and capable light, which would also require us to take more responsibility for choosing what we perceive. Then we would come full circle in understanding that *we are what we perceive.* If we could alter our perceptions we could also alter the objective world around us. During my psychic surgery, I could feel, more than at any other time, that the act of my perception itself helped form the perceived event and was an integral part of it.

My perception of my own identity had been so limited that I was skeptical of an event that spoke to a more expanded reality. Perhaps I had felt more comfortable with my limited perception of myself because everything outside of that limitation seemed foreign, alien, and frightening to me and I would rather have gone with the devil I knew than the angel I was capable of knowing.

If my body is made up of molecules determined by my consciousness to take the human form and all of it is actually composed of immortal God-like energy, I can accept the concept that psychic surgery is performed through a spiritual connection with the Divine by separating the living atoms one from another with an energy that doesn't violate, but simply and gently slips *through* the physical, much as a hand slips gently, without violation, through liquid.

I don't need a scientist to tell me it's true or false. I know it because it happened to me. And, as Einstein concluded at the end of his life, "Knowledge is experience. Anything else is just information."

After Ojai, Chris Griscom asked Alex to heal at her Light Institute in Galisteo, New Mexico.

I invited a nationally respected surgeon I knew to view the procedure for himself. I will call him Dr. Theodore Bennett in order to protect his privacy. Ted was interested in my mystical/spiritual learning but obviously kept an objective and balanced eye on all of it.

Bennett met Orbito, heard the explanation of his healing, and began to ask more questions.

It was clear to Bennett from the outset that Orbito was describing a different kind of medical science. Orbito understood that most traditionally well-trained doctors had difficulty in understanding that there might be an invisible truth just as profound and effective as a visible truth. Yet, while there have been colossal advances in science and medicine in the last 150 years, there are many things that we cannot understand or explain by resorting to laboratory formulae.

Orbito said that he didn't view medical science as a limited science, but more that he saw it simply as a systemized knowledge of laws and facts concerning the physical world, which we already understand. He rather hoped that those who taught the physical sciences would soon include and embrace the deep knowledge of the spiritual and metaphysical world in their training of others.

In fact, in his view, Orbito felt there were two grand divisions in science: that of the physical or material world with a scientific system of laws to govern and understand it, and that of a spiritual dimension that belonged to the invisible world, which also contained its own scientific system and laws to govern and understand it.

Up to now, he said, man has become proficient in the mastering of the visible and material sciences, but mastery of science and technology without an understanding of the spiritual force in nature would always lead to negative results—the creation of planet-threatening weaponry, of heavy industrialization at the cost of health and even lives; whereas embracing the sciences that deal with the impact of the "invisible" on our world would put mankind in touch with the power of spiritual energy so that it could work *with* technology. Orbito said it wasn't his intention to replace traditional medical therapy, but more to enhance and complement it. He explained that further by saying that when an ailment falls into the material field, a medical therapy could be applied, but when an ailment is within the province of the spiritual realm, such as so-called psychosomatic diseases, then spiritual healing could be used: healing itself involves both body and spirit, and one is not mutually exclusive of the other. Orbito told Bennett that in his view, all healing, be it medical or spiritual, is a therapeutic practice ordained by God as a means through which physical and spiritual equilibrium may be achieved. The art of healing then provides man with the means to correct any imbalance in someone's physiological as well as spiritual constitution. In the end, though, he said that he believed that *spiritual therapy is the core of medical therapy*. That without the spiritual element, medicine loses its impact, its sacredness, and its meaning. Since human life is sacred, preserving it is a holy act.

He went on to explain that down through the ages healing was thought of as an act of the Divine. To underscore that truth, there was a time in history when healing was the major function of religious leaders. In fact, the Oath of Hippocrates was a physician's prayer enunciating the sanctity of the art of healing. Similarly today, when physicians perform healing, they are indulging in a holy act, partaking of something Divine.

Medical therapy then should be gaining spiritual nobility, Orbito said. Instead, we have become so technologically oriented and drug seduced that the profession of healing has itself taken a turn toward destruction. The natural laws of man, nature, and energy are being ignored; something must be done soon to include the participation of the patient and God in the healing process.

He concluded by saying that that was what he felt spiritual therapy was ordained to accomplish.

"A clash of doctrines is not a disaster—it is an opportunity," said Alfred North Whitehead, the British mathematician and philosopher, and Orbito liked to quote him.

Bennett questioned Orbito about the debunkers, the scientific experimental observations, the power that he felt he had, and so on. Orbito said that he was only an instrument. "I am a human being like anyone else, but when I'm doing my healing, I am an instrument of God . . . without the aid of the Divine province, I cannot do anything."

The most important thing I heard Alex say was, "The primary mission of spiritual healing is not the elimination of physical ailments, but to promote inner awareness, a sense of spiritual attachment, and a personal fellowship with God."

Bennett listened respectfully, forming no judgments, and then proceeded to observe a series of operations. He stood beside Orbito and peered into people's bodies, which he was used to viewing from a different vantage point in his own operating room. Here there was no anesthesia, no instruments, no pain, no postoperative shock, no more than ten minutes per operation, and, as far as he could see, no blood capsules, no chicken gizzards, and no sleight-of-hand.

Bennett had difficulty assessing what he had seen. "I saw it and I don't understand it," he said. "It is mind-boggling. I know we have a great deal more to learn. I simply don't understand."

Several other things happened while Bennett was witnessing the operations.

Alex opened up my abdomen and placed a large gauze pad inside. He then removed his hands and the wound closed up with the gauze remaining inside. He did a healing meditation over me for about three minutes, claiming the gauze was collecting negative vibrations, the absence of which would advance my energies. Then he opened up my upper chest and withdrew the gauze that had been placed in my abdomen! It was full of clotted blood. He withdrew his hands.

He claims that the left hand always controls the material plane and must be present *within* the patient at all times to prevent pain. The right hand controls the spiritual plane, which he uses for attracting the negative coagulation produced by stress and thought forms of negativity.

Bennett listened and tried to make it compute in his traditional understanding.

In the meantime, something happened I will never forget.

I was talking with Alex while he operated on another friend of mine whose abdomen was open. Suddenly Alex took my right hand in his right hand. He closed his eyes and concentrated intensely. "Concentrate on God," he said to me. "I will now show you what I experience while operating."

I concentrated on love and light and everything else that God represents to me. Alex's left hand remained in my friend's abdomen. After a few minutes Orbito took my right hand and held it above my friend's abdomen. "Now put your hand into his body," he commanded gently. I thought I'd pass out.

"It is all right," Alex said. "You have the Divine current running in your hand now. Please go ahead, you will learn something for your own understanding."

I summoned up my courage, in much the same way you prepare to touch anything unfamiliar. I looked down at my friend. He shrugged his shoulders (he couldn't feel anything anyway), and with Alex's right hand guiding mine, I put my hand into his abdominal wall. It was a moment that will live with me always. My hand was inside his abdomen up to my wrist and I felt absolutely nothing physical! In fact, the feeling had a dreamlike quality to it. It was as though I had plunged my hand into a warm mist. It simply made no logical sense. I tried to comprehend what I was feeling. "This is how it is for me," Orbito said. "I never feel anything physical. The body is only 'thought.' It is only what we imagine it to be. It has no density when the current of the Divine is running through it."

As soon as I felt doubt, disbelief, and questions ripple intensely through my mind, Alex removed my hand. "Such thoughts will affect the patient," he warned. "That is why I pray and meditate for three hours every morning, so that my trust and connection is strong and unwavering."

I removed my hand and looked at it. There was moisture covering it, but no blood. It was as though my hand had a mind and spirit of its own, unconnected to my brain. It had experienced something separate from me, as though it had been connected to Alex's mind, not mine!

Alex claimed that whenever he sat down to meditate in order to operate and heal, he could feel the Divine force descend upon him, causing a cold sensation in his arms and fingers. They become energized with this magnetic force, which enables him to separate molecules of the flesh without using incising instruments.

Sometimes he uses no "surgery," but rather heals only by touching.

Whatever was going on in Ted Bennett's mind was as interesting to me as the phenomenon itself. "This makes me feel that the body itself is a trick," he said. "A physical trick that we play on ourselves in order to experience life, or something. Or, is Orbito the trick?"

I could feel Ted's confusion. Had I suggested he come to New Mexico to witness a sophisticated sleight-of-hand act? Had we both been fooled?

After a few days with Orbito, Bennett didn't say much. We'd have meals together but I could feel him deliberately avoiding the subject. He seemed not only to be sifting the information he was witnessing, but somehow he was evaluating what he thought of me for placing him in such an untenable position. Was he embarrassed, perhaps, because he felt *I* was deluded? I found that I didn't know what to say. I felt Ted back away from discussing anything with me. He took walks alone in the desert. He had seen Orbito's hands in people's bodies. He had smelled and seen the blood. He had stood behind, in front of, and closely beside this "spiritual surgeon" from the Philippines. He had studied Orbito's work with expert eyes, yet he could find nothing that evidenced fraud or fakery. In fact, Bennett had said that the human body, not the surgery, seemed to be the illusion.

"I'm very uncomfortable with what I'm seeing," he said. "I can't understand. I have spent my life training in medical science, yet what I am seeing seems to make a mockery of that."

As a result of Bennett's genuine philosophical quandary, I realized the significance of what I had done. I had invited him here and he had trusted me enough to come. Yet, I had called into play and exposed him, almost as a metaphysical lark, to invisible truths and forces of nature which, by their very existence, defied scientific explanation. I had almost playfully knocked the traditional pins out from under his support system. Confronted with something inexplicable in terms of present empirical knowledge, such an intelligent, caring, and rational person required a personal patience in the face of his own confusion, to say nothing of the required appreciation of wider and deeper truths—truths that science might somehow suspect existed but couldn't countenance yet in a responsible manner. The challenge for Ted, then, was to respect that there were finer perspectives in everything within which a more subtle science of understanding would someday be acknowledged. On top of all that, I had forced him to take responsibility for what he had seen. This, I believe, was the most stressful aspect of it all. If the psychic surgery wasn't a trick, then what was it?

By the time Bennett left New Mexico, he hadn't reached a solution in his own mind or within his own system of truth. I have not discussed it with him since. More than anything, *I* began to take more seriously my responsibility in exposing people to phenomena that completely upset their personal sense of reality. Spiritual technology is not a game. It isn't a parlor adventure to entertain, or a divertissement. It is a serious and profound recognition that there are energies and forces at work in the universe that lie waiting to be accessed so that the human race can heal itself into a more spiritual state of truth and being.

I, in the meantime, cannot forget the feeling of my hand inside my friend's abdomen with absolutely no trace of physicality other than the sensation of moistness.

Many times I also need to remind myself of Buddha's contention that life itself in the physical dimension is really an illusion. If that is true, then we can create this illusion to be anything we desire. *That* is the responsibility difficult to accept.

16

Childlike Pursuit

*The grandest of things are achieved with a
light heart: allow your soul to smile.*

From the time I was twelve years old I wanted to know how the universe worked and the role I played in it. The two questions were intertwined in my mind.

I had the notion that if I knew what made me, I would know more about what made the universe and vice versa. Therefore, the identity of the universe would help explain me. And the more I could find out about me, the more the universe would make sense.

The lofty dreams and questions common to many adolescents certainly don't qualify them as mystics, but later—and the more I read of the musings of the physicists on the subject of the origins of the universe—the more *they* did indeed sound like mystics.

I wanted to know about what started it all and how it happened. So did they. I wanted to know, indeed believe, that there was a harmony at work.

They were seeking the same answer. Einstein said that "the most incomprehensible thing about the universe is that it is comprehensible." Such a glorious riddle.

Why was it that we human beings could see, sense, and dream the truths of the great unknown out there without having to be told?

Were we remembering? Were we inextricably woven into it? Were we perhaps made up of the same "mind stuff"?

In the spirit of that question, I wanted to meet a person who had struck my heart and mind from the first moment I saw a picture of him, Professor Stephen Hawking of Cambridge University in England. To identify him as the brilliant professor of physics and mathematics who, among many other things, significantly enlarged our understanding of "black holes" is simply to belittle the meaning of his life in this world. His smile is more to the point of his real identity.

He was writing a book aptly titled *A Brief History of Time: From the Big Bang to Black Holes*. I knew his editor, asked for a meeting with Hawking, and arranged to meet him in Cambridge.

It was a rainy English day. I had just finished shooting *Madame Sousatzka* in London and was looking forward with eager anticipation to the long-awaited meeting. The logistics of the journey to Cambridge, however, proved to be as complicated as the questions in my mind.

My car had been impounded because it blocked traffic in front of the house where I was staying. A totally unrelated traffic jam caused me to miss the train, and when, after a two-hour wait, I finally boarded another, I arrived in Cambridge to find that the cabdriver at the train station didn't know the address I had been given. I was beginning to wonder if my meeting with Hawking was simply not meant to be.

All of that changed when I found him in a restaurant surrounded by his students at a buffet lunch.

I saw the wheelchair first, together with his attending nurse. I had been warned that his initial appearance would shock me because his frail body was almost entirely paralyzed by Lou Gehrig's disease and he could move only one finger on each hand and had great difficulty even breathing. What I hadn't been prepared for was the radiance and sheer happiness of his face and most particularly his smile. I felt tears prick in my eyes, not of pity but of a great, welling love. I couldn't understand why.

Since he couldn't talk, as a result of his tracheotomy, he communicated with his two good fingers on a computer that was attached to his wheelchair. When he looked up and saw me, he spelled out on his computer, "You are very pretty, would you like a first course for lunch or do you want to go immediately to the entree!?" Clearly not a man to waste time or words but willing to gently fulfill polite social appropriateness.

I mumbled something about food not mattering to me as much as meeting him, whereupon he went on to spell out something else. Immediately the computer translated his written words to a robotical voice box that talked! "Please excuse my American accent!" it said. And indeed it had an American accent, because it had been invented and programmed two years previously by a computer expert from Sunnyvale, California.

Hawking smiled at me again. "Sometimes my voice changes," he said on the computer, which again translated the words to speech. "When I'm angry, either my voice changes or I run over my students with my wheelchair."

I laughed out loud but I was profoundly confused by his capacity for such happiness in the face of his personal physical tragedy. And then I caught myself. Happiness or sorrow had apparently been a choice for him. Hawking had clearly made up his mind to cope with his reality.

His nurse gently scooped food into his mouth. His ability to swallow is minimal, but the dribbles onto his chin and tie seemed irrelevant and even humorous. He watched me carefully and must have caught something of my feelings, for his two fingers moved quickly to spell out something else. The words on the computer screen appeared before the voice was activated. "It matters that you just don't give up," he said. He continued to gaze at me intently as he waited for my reaction. I blinked and sat down.

I needed to assimilate what had occurred to me in the first two minutes of meeting a human being who seemed to relate to the betrayal of his body as an inconvenience that had not very much to do with the state of his spirit. And on top of that I had never been in the presence of anyone who exuded so much love. This was a physics professor, a mathematician, a scientific skeptic, a person who had stated publicly that he believed in nothing that could not be proved? As I was beginning to realize more and more in my life, people cannot be categorized. I wondered what the rest of the day would produce.

An oval-faced, kindly, youngish woman next to me took my hand. "I'm Stephen's wife," she said. "We are so glad you could make it. Let's get you some food."

She seemed so down-to-earth and practical. But as the lunch progressed, the introductions to the students were accomplished, and the conversation deepened, I realized that the interplay between Stephen (he insisted I call him by his first name) and his wife, Jane, was much the same as that of any couple; the bond intense, the love and respect apparent, and the barriers of nurses, wheelchairs, and paralysis insignificant inconveniences.

I don't remember who made the initial foray into the discussion of "truth beyond what is provable." I honestly don't think it was I. In any case, Jane said she was often frustrated with Stephen and his scientific approach to truth because she felt that there was an explanation for life that lay in the lap of the Gods and the heart.

"I don't like mysticism," Stephen said via his voice-box computer. "But my wife and I don't always agree." He smiled at her and then at me. "But I need the heart because physics isn't everything."

He hesitated a moment and then said, "I need heart *and* physics, but I believe that when I die, I die, and it will be finished."

Hawking's disease began when he was in his twenties. He said that meeting and falling in love with Jane had enabled him to proceed in his life with hope, and that he could live with the knowledge that his life could end at any given moment as long as he could continue to work.

He had written *A Brief History of Time* for the "popular consciousness" because he wanted to have an "airport book out there on the racks, a book people can pick up in airports and read on planes," he said. He saw no reason why advanced physics wouldn't be popular if explained simply. "I can prove the last fifteen billion years," he said without mischievousness, "so I dictated it on my computer, which took almost as long as what I proved, which was only a brief moment in either case." Then he smiled and again waited for my reaction.

His students seemed to be used to purity of confidence in these sweeping statements. Given that Hawking is acknowledged to have a mind of such incandescent brilliance that there is no way to assess its potential, this is hardly surprising. He could well be privy to dimensions beyond the reality of the physical world the rest of us inhabit.

"Do you like my accent?" he asked via the robot computer. I nodded, shrugged, and said yes in a qualified way. His face lit up and he went on to say that he had a new computer back in his office, which he was longing to experiment with.

Jane, the nurse, and his students understood that this was the cue to bring the luncheon to a close. Stephen pushed the control button on his motorized wheelchair with one of his good fingers and, like a mechanical human top, he spun his vehicle around on itself and headed out the door of the restaurant. His students barely acknowledged this maneuver, electing instead to discuss among themselves the nature of entropy, knowing that he would run over them anyway. Stephen's nurse ran after him. Jane took a phone call, and I was left with the choice of running after the nurse and Stephen, discussing the second law of thermodynamics with the students, or waiting for Jane to get off the phone. I decided to run.

The restaurant was on the third floor of the building, which meant that Stephen needed to guide himself into an elevator and descend three floors. He arrived at the elevator and propelled his chair into it just in time for the door to close in his nurse's face. I could see he was playing a game.

She sighed and bounded down the stairs, with the

clear intention of meeting him on the ground floor. I followed, chuckling in disbelief at the antics of Stephen Hawking playing hide-and-seek.

The nurse of course was late. So was I. The people in the lobby of the building stopped in awe as they watched Hawking speed by them and out the door to charge into the quiet cobblestone streets of Cambridge. The nurse flew after him. I flew after her. Stephen had wheels and a motor, so there was really no contest. And he knew it. He proceeded to guide his chair on and off the curb in a kind of undulating wavy motion, spicing his choreography with a little pirouette every now and then. Cars slowed down, of course, but apparently saw no reason to stop because the hometown intellectual community knew that their mad professor was simply out busting loose again.

Apart from everything else, what really appealed to my sense of theater was that this entire episode was taking place in the rain! The slippery cobblestones glistened with moisture and I was hard put to keep from falling as the nurse and I (she was wearing rubber-soled shoes, I was not) tore after Stephen, who was, no doubt, perfectly comfortable in the knowledge that he had nonslip tires on his wheelchair.

A mile and much gasping laughter later, the nurse and I straggled into Stephen's office at the university. He was waiting for us with a glowing face and an innocently teasing smile.

Stephen's secretary felt that nothing out of the ordinary had occurred, and simply inquired whether he wanted to play with his computer now or later. His answer was a resounding *Now*.

So the nurse and I dutifully followed Stephen into his office to watch a further display of his childlike exuberance.

My first visual impression as I entered his office was clutter. Clutter of books and papers lying about on his desk and on all the tabletops and on shelves that reached to the ceiling. On his desk there was also a container filled to overflowing with papers. Hanging on the wall was a simple picture of Albert Einstein. Stephen guided his chair to an imposing position behind his desk.

"Look under the papers," he said. Rather tentatively I began to riffle through them.

"What am I looking for?" I asked. He smiled. I continued to look. Nothing seemed to be in order. There were calculus equations or advanced mathematics of some kind scribbled on page after page.

"Fifteen billion years," he stated.

"Fifteen billion years of what?" I asked.

"Time," he answered.

Then I realized that this was his oblique way of telling me his manuscript was under there. I found it.

"Take it," he said. "I can write another." I choked. "Take it and you'll see my corrections in the margins. Tell me if you think this is an airport book."

I lifted the precious manuscript papers from the mess and held the untidy packet in my hands.

"I can't do that," I answered. "I'll wait and read it when you're finished. This belongs in a museum somewhere."

"All right," he said matter-of-factly, and with that he spelled out how he had written the book on his computer. He described how the machinery enabled him to carry on with his teaching, lecturing, and so on. As he was outlining the process to me, a teen-aged girl entered the room. He looked up at her and pure love poured through his eyes. They began to carry on a conversation in computer-voice short-hand. The subject had something to do with where she was going that night. This was his daughter, and the interpersonal communication between father and child could have been straight from *The Cosby Show*. He wanted to know what time she'd be home and whom she was going to be with. He teased her, and in the end whatever permission she asked him for was granted. She left happy and bouncy.

I wanted to ask him what it felt like to be him, but instead I heard myself say, "When you close your eyes what do you see?"

Without hesitation he answered, "You mean the universe or beautiful women?"

I chuckled. "Aren't they the same thing?" I answered.

"Oh," he said, "I don't know which has more curves!"

With that he spun his chair around from behind his desk and charged out of the office. "The computer I'm going to play with is next door," said the mechanical voice as he and his chair exited.

The nurse and I followed. He led us into a small room where two of his students who were playing with some advanced computer screen deferentially peeled away to allow space for their professor.

Stephen abruptly brought his chair to a halt with a flourish and gazed at the technological marvel in front of him.

"This is my new toy," he said. "I am really an eight-year-old boy at heart." An unnecessary evaluation if ever there was one. "This is not only user-friendly but user-cuddly," he went on. I wondered what language he had used in his "airport" book.

In an apparently sudden switch he said, "I have my ups and downs." And repeated, "It matters if you don't just give up."

I was suddenly aware of how important this "toy" was to his survival. He reveled in its potential possibilities.

"These toys will someday be able to do everything but fall in love," he mused. "And they are clever because they don't need to have sex to reproduce."

I was beginning to wonder about Professor Stephen Hawking in a much more personal way. Just as I thought about having some bawdy fun with him, he launched into the discussion that I had hoped for all along.

"Humans," he began, "evolved in certain conditions about one million years ago. Conditions are very different now."

That was all I needed. "*Are* we evolving then?" I asked. "Or are we going to destroy ourselves?"

"There's quite a chance we will destroy ourselves," he answered, which I thought was an interesting way to put it. "Evolution is very slow. The Greeks would have understood our science."

"But," I asked, "will conditions change again so that maybe our behavior can change also?"

He tapped out a firm answer. "Conditions *will* change if we don't destroy ourselves first. But we still behave like primitive tribes."

"Would the threat of destruction motivate that change?" I asked.

"It doesn't seem to have had much effect so far, you know," he said. "When you understand the scale of the universe, human quarrels seem petty."

"Yes," I answered, wondering what it would be like to understand what he understood.

"The universe," he went on, "and everything in it can be explained by well-defined laws."

"You mean then there are no accidents?" I asked.

"Correct."

"Then is our behavior also part of well-defined laws?" I asked.

"No," he answered. "Our behavior is part of our human nature, which evolved in certain conditions."

"And we have inherited that?"

"Yes."

I thought I was beginning to understand something. "Would you call the universe a loving place?" I asked. "I mean, you said everything could be explained by well-defined laws."

"Yes."

"Well then, that means the universe operates within a harmony, doesn't it?"

"Yes."

"Well, isn't harmonic energy loving?"

"I don't know," he answered, "that there is anything loving about energy. I don't think *loving* is a word I could ascribe to the universe."

"What is a word you *could* use?"

He thought for a moment. "Order," he said. "The universe is well-defined order."

"So the question becomes how we define order in relation to how we see ourselves and our behavior?"

"Maybe," he answered. "What do you mean?"

"Well," I began. I hesitated in order to think my way through my thought. "Since we are all afraid that chaos may be the natural state of life, you could say that belief in universal order could produce feelings of love, whereas a belief in chaos could produce destruction. In other words, we define ourselves by what we believe the 'natural' state of the universe to be and we see our fellow man accordingly."

"I don't see the connection," he answered.

"Well," I went on, "if we feel the universe is a dangerous chaotic place, we feel threatened by everything it produces, including our fellow human beings;

maybe that's why our behavior is chaotic, threatened, and primitive. In other words, we behave in direct ratio to how we see the universe. And since the job of science is to explain the universe to the common man, you scientists hold 'reality' as a hostage for the rest of us." Stephen looked up at me intently. "So," I said, "if you would tell us that the universe is harmonic and well ordered, perhaps we would see ourselves in that same light."

He smiled. "So far we have not been too successful in eliminating crime," he answered.

"Maybe you guys haven't gone far enough in *believing* in harmony. I mean, what is the purpose of your scientific investigation?"

He looked at me from his chair. He didn't respond.

"I mean, doesn't science exist as a method to investigate God?"

Stephen pushed a button on his wheelchair and spun it around.

"Come," he said.

He led me back into his office. I followed him. His nurse followed both of us. He steered his wheelchair to his desk.

"Look at that wall," he directed. I walked over to what looked like a framed cartoon hanging behind his desk.

Stephen smiled at me. I looked more closely. The cartoonist had drawn caricatures of Hawking and of another scientist named Hartle standing in front of a blackboard plastered with complex equations and symbols. Intently the two men studied the figures. The caption had Stephen talking. He said, "No doubt about it, Hartle, we've mathematically expressed the purpose of the universe. Gad, how I love the thrill of scientific discovery."

I chuckled at the cartoon and then I turned back to Stephen and said, "Now this would really have been funny if the cartoonist had had you saying, '*God,* how I love the thrill of scientific discovery' instead of *Gad.*"

I had meant to be casually quippy with my remark but Stephen didn't take it that way. He looked into my eyes for a good solid minute. Then a beatific expression melted across his face. His fingers began to operate his computer until the mechanical voice said, "The man who did this cartoon may have known my work, but he didn't know me."

I felt myself gasp. I didn't want to trivialize the moment by saying anything. I just gazed at him. Stephen continued to look unwaveringly at me. The gentle intensity coming from him was so moving that I found it almost embarrassing. Then Stephen tapped out a message. "Come here and give me a kiss," he directed.

I walked over to him and leaned down over his frail body. "Do you have an open marriage?" I teased.

His face beamed. "I expect so," he answered. "Perhaps we could go to the movies together."

We spent the rest of the afternoon talking about "regular" subjects. He wanted to know how I made "magic in films" and I wanted to know how he viewed the magic of life. "Same question," he concluded. "Same pursuit."

Yet not for a moment did he concede that within himself or me or anyone else lay the secret of universal reality. I didn't press my twelve-year-old belief. I didn't have to. For me he was living proof that a childlike sense of wonder nurtured an exquisite sense of inner peace that surpassed all understanding.

He was himself the proof that the harmony he exuded was derived from his own understanding of the harmony in the universe he had investigated and proved.

I promised I'd take him to my movie when I returned to England. He promised we had a date.

As I left his office I vowed to sustain my twelve-year-old convictions. If he was an example of how that worked, it would seem to be not only the happiest of decisions but probably the wisest and most practical.

CODA

Science and God?

———————— ✦ ————————

Without beginning, the Law creates.

If, as Hawking and many other scientists say, the Big Bang explosion resulted in life as we know it today, then the seeds of all things, ourselves included, were present at the birth of creation, and every scrap of matter and energy and blood and bones and thought present in the cosmos today could be traced back to the origins of the universe from one small subatomic particle of light. That makes us each sparks of the same light. It also makes each of us a hologram of the entire event. The energies that fragmented and separated and multiplied as the young universe expanded and cooled continue to operate in the beating of our hearts and the movements of our bodies, as well as in the alignment and behavior of the stars. We and they— all things and everything are a connected whole. That is the meaning of "We are *one*." The evolution of the universe, then, is continuing not only around us but within us. Our thoughts, our dreams, and our awareness are part of that universe, the physical and the spiritual inextricably bound together.

Science says it owes a great deal to religion and the spiritual point of view. Modern science began with the rediscovery in the Renaissance of the old Greek idea that nature is rationally intelligent. A simple system ruled by a single set of laws. Many physicists are now saying that everything that is or can be, was contained within that first single spark of energy, rapidly expanding and ruled by a single primordial law.

What is that law and where did *it* come from? Are scientists suggesting that everything may come from and return to a dimension and a time and space about which we know nothing?

Of one thing they say they can be certain. That first light-time-spark that created the universe was the first *cause* creating the effect of expansion. The laws of cause and effect then continued to create evolution. But, as Thomas Aquinas pondered, "If we could but find the first effect, we would come closer to finding the first cause . . . which is God." How odd that when confronted with proof of supernal power, the main problem should be what to call it!

Science says nothing preceded the spark of light that preceded the universe because it cannot be traced. Mystics say God preceded the spark of light, that God motivated the spark to ignite into matter, that God is a giant consciousness that cannot be measured or even conceived of because it *is*, literally, everything.

In the absence of knowledge of the origins of the spark of light, the primary question for science is: how can there be a universe created out of nothing? Why is there *something* instead of *nothing*?

There is a prayer I used to read as a child:

> *Great is God, our Lord. Great is his power, and there is no end to his wisdom. Praise Him, you heaven, and glorify Him sun and moon, and you planets. For out of Him, through Him, and in Him are all things. Every perception and every knowledge.*

That prayer was written in the seventeenth century, not by a priest or a mystic, but by an astronomer, Johannes Kepler, who discovered the laws that govern the motion of the planets.

In fact, the founding fathers of modern science—Kepler, Copernicus, Isaac Newton, and Galileo—were, by and large, profoundly spiritual men. They *wanted* to believe in an impeccable harmony. Modern scientific research is now close to proving that all creation is ruled by an elegant and single principle. The Grand Unification Theory. The principle of God light? The principle of beauty? The principle of harmony? They say that the universe operates and evolves according to the law of cause and effect; that the universe is nonchaotic. It has symmetry and explicable behavior patterns. It is, as Einstein said, "comprehensible." And it is continuing to expand. Therefore, the comprehension is continuing to expand.

To me this relates to human consciousness and my twelve-year-old theory that *I* and the universe were one.

Einstein and the American astronomer Edwin Hubbell concluded that the galaxies are not expanding into a space that is already there, but rather that space itself is expanding, carrying the galaxies with it. To use a balloon as an analogy: if I painted dots on the surface of a balloon and then blew it up, I would see each of the dots moving away from one another as the balloon expands. If I put *myself* on one of the dots, *I* become the center of the round balloon and all the other dots move around and away from me. If I let the air out of the balloon, all the dots come toward my dot until they form the ground point of zero, where all dots are in one place at one time. If I blew it up again, my dot would be the center of the expansion. Yet, everyone else on any other dot would also experience themselves as the center of the expansion *and* the collapse of the balloon. Every dot, then, and every place on the balloon is the center of expansion. The analogy is that we are each the center of a universe that itself is expanding. We are carried with it, and the more consciously aware we are of the expansion, the more we are attuned to the acceleration and movement itself. Therefore, the more aware we are of ourselves, the more aware we are of the universe *because,* as the expanding balloon proves, *from the beginning we each are the universe before and after it expands.*

What is the center of the universe? Every place is the center. Who is the center? *Everyone* is the center. Where is God? God, and the energy from which all has been created, is in everything, because we have all inherited that first instant in time when it first began.

Here we are, then, alive in space with the memory, on some level, of having been born about fifteen billion years ago. We can't see our past, but we can *feel* it. It is a part of our consciousness. It is a part of our physicality. It is our heritage. It is who we are. It is where we have been, and where we are going.

By looking at nature on a scale of subatomic structures of matter and energy and the fundamental forces that govern the behavior of subatomic particles, we see that they are each reflecting particles of light. Light that reflects a grandeur and a beauty and an extraordinary power that from the beginning created what we now call human history, and indeed the history of the cosmos. From a single kernel of light particle comes everything there is: the hydrogen, the helium, the photons, atoms, protons, electrons, neutrons. Science and physics and Stephen Hawking have traced the universe back to a time when it was about ten to the minus thirty-fifth of a second old. The explosion just after the countdown contact of "nothing" moving on to "something." What went before is the mystery.

Perhaps as we "go within" ourselves we will sense the answer to that "something." Perhaps that is indeed the riddle. We have been looking outside for the answers. Perhaps they have resided all along in the vast interior of our own individual consciousness, which *knows* it is somehow attached to the grand motivator. The inspiration of science itself has come from the spiritual belief in one God—one Source. Perhaps Alex Orbito and Gasparetto and Mauricio have simply attuned themselves to a more refined knowledge of their source, and we are each capable of such physical phenomena if we integrate the spiritually intuitive memory of who we really are. Perhaps *that* was what I was seeing in Stephen Hawking's eyes and could describe it with no other word but *love*. Maybe the more we go within ourselves with love, using the techniques and age-old procedures of color and energy and sound, the more we simply remember who we are and come away enlightened with the truth that *we were all there at the beginning*. We are therefore one. We are each therefore part of God. We are each therefore *naturally* harmonious, and our individual recognition of that harmony is in direct ratio to how deeply we recognize and accept the God within ourselves. With that profound realization perhaps we can trust the loving and well-ordered magic of who we are meant to be and get out of our own way and create our lives accordingly.

ABOUT THE AUTHOR

SHIRLEY MACLAINE was born and raised in Virginia. She began her career as a Broadway dancer and singer, then progressed to featured performer and award-winning actress in television and films. She has traveled extensively around the world, and her experiences in Africa, Bhutan, and the Far East formed the basis for her first two bestsellers, *"Don't Fall Off the Mountain"* and *You Can Get There from Here*. Her investigations into the spiritual realm were the focus of *Out on a Limb, Dancing in the Light,* and *It's All In the Playing*, all of which were national and worldwide bestsellers.

One of the most remarkable personal odysseys of the twentieth century, come, enter Shirley MacLaine's universe and live the journey inward . . .

"I have been having an extraordinary adventure for the past seven years," says MacLaine in the opening of GOING WITHIN, where she takes the reader on an unprecedented and revealing journey into their inner self, a journey she herself sought, then shared in her impressive collection of bestsellers.

DON'T FALL OFF THE MOUNTAIN

In 1970, Shirley MacLaine surprised the world with her candid and unusual autobiography, proving herself to be more than a great actress, but an outspoken thinker and a keen observer as well. Tracing the path from her Virginia roots to Hollywood stardom, she invites the reader to a moving and humorous celebration of life.

THE BIGGEST SURPRISE brought by success was that suddenly people were interested in what I thought, not because I was older—I was still in my twenties—or because I knew what I was doing, but because I made $800,000 a picture. It was suddenly O.K. for me to call Samuel Goldwyn "Sam," and William Wyler "Willy." They had been people with a Mr. before their names when I was young-and-nobody, but now that stardom was mine I had become *somebody* and we could communicate as equals.

Success in Hollywood forced me to come face to face with certain things: young or not, ready or not, success forced me to evaluate myself.

Take money for instance. Before Hollywood, I had never had more than fifty dollars I could call "spendable." True, I had never lacked the money for necessities—food and a place to sleep—but luxury money was unknown to me. Now suddenly I had all the luxury money I wanted, but I still acted as though I had only the fifty dollars. I shopped in bargain basements and more often than not bought nothing. Several times I found myself haggling over something that had a fixed price, finally paying the money and leaving the purchase behind on the counter. I felt guilty because I could have what I wanted. I was reluctant to indulge myself, even though I had worked hard for it and economic security had become a reality.

I also found I wanted success and recognition without losing my anonymity. I was haunted by my psychological conditioning as a child to be inconspicuous. It was impossible. I had to adjust to shocking, baseless adulation and an enraging loss of privacy.

Unreasonably, I resented the attention I attracted even though I had fought for it. The most pleasant strangers provoked my fury because they simply looked at me, or watched how I picked up a fork, or stared while I spoke quietly with my daughter, or told me that they had seen the same facial expression on the screen. I felt that it was not their right to stare or to be interested in me. I was wrong, but regardless of how full of admiration their interest might be, I still resented it. I resented my enforced and constant awareness of self; I didn't want to live in a world of only "me."

At first, I reacted with stony hostility, hardly smiling when someone approached me with a compliment. For a while I denied that I was Shirley MacLaine—and I always felt ashamed afterward. After all, how could I call it an invasion of privacy when I had chosen to splash myself across the screen, seeking the applause and approval and attention of strangers?

But I did. I wanted to stand in a supermarket line again with people who were unaware of being observed. I wanted to hear the snatches of personal conversation, notice the way people dressed, the attitudes of their children, and observe the interplay between those who seemed happily married and between those who were miserable. It was all part of what had kept me alive, and it was gone.

I wanted to splash in the waves at Malibu again with Steve and Sachie without being stared at by passersby. Suddenly I felt exposed in a bathing suit, acutely conscious of my white skin that wouldn't tan, embarrassed by my masses of freckles, afraid that my figure might not be what people expected. "Is your mother Shirley MacLaine?" people would ask Sachie. And Sachie would say, "Yes, but she says she's really Shirley Parker." And then she would ask me, "Why are you so special, Mom?" And I would try to explain that I wasn't really special—it was my work that was special. And she would say, "I wish they would leave us alone so we could play again."

But the stardom I had fought for meant that "they" would not leave me alone again. And of course I didn't really want them to. I wanted to be wanted. I needed to be appreciated. I did what I did to win their approval. Behind all my resentment, I was terrified that I would disappoint them.

Instinctively I knew that, if I wanted to maintain an honest level in my work, I would have to remain vulnerable inside myself. If I built a shell and crawled into it, I would fail. People want to see reflections of true human feelings—their own. An actor can only hope to be a mirror of humanity, a mirror to be looked into by audiences. My problem was how to keep myself vulnerable and sensitive while remaining resilient. How to be tough and tender.

As my new values emerged I began to realize that I had *power*. Money was one thing, fame and recognition another; both had to be dealt with. But to feel power was devastating.

I found myself with the power to hire and fire people, to impose my opinions on others—to be listened to. What did I think of so-and-so? Did I like his story and the way it was written? Would I accept so-and-so as my director? So-and-so needs a job; would I accept him as costar or collaborator?

I found myself making decisions because they were part of my new responsibility. Sometimes my decision would wreck the life of someone I'd never met. Although I didn't want to express my opinion—I had never really learned to respect my own opinion because I always believed someone else knew better—I was forced to because I was a *star*. And stars, for some reason, are supposed to know. If they don't, they're supposed to act as though they do.

The power of my position changed the people I had known before. Some who had been direct and honest became wary—wary of offending in my presence, and anxious to be assured of my respect and high evaluation. Others, reacting, became my harshest critics, afraid I might think they were kowtowing to me. I tried to put my old acquaintances at ease, to let them know that nothing basic in me had changed. And I was distressed to discover that often it was they whom I had changed. My success was too much for them. They couldn't handle it. I wondered what they would be like if success had happened to them instead of to me.

And as Shirley herself says of her first book, "I learned to spread my wings as a young artist and began to take charge of my personal destiny. . . . I reached out to touch the unknown—and was changed by it."

YOU CAN GET THERE FROM HERE

*These are the tumultuous years, where her changing life contin-
ued to evolve, where Shirley MacLaine discovered that "anything is possible."*

*From her first taste of professional disaster to her impassioned
political efforts . . . to her emergence as an important voice in
the international women's movement . . . to her life-affirming
odyssey to the People's Republic of China, this is the unforgettable story of a crisis in self-doubt to a joyous new stage in her
life.*

LET ME START at the end: in Las Vegas. It was twenty
after eight on July 12, 1974. I stood in the wings of the giant
hotel theater set in the starkness of the American desert. I heard
the roll of tympani, and then the strains of the theme from *The
Apartment*. There were no more minutes left, either for delay or
for thought or for hesitation. An oddly detached voice called my
name. I walked out on stage, and started to sing:

> *If they could see me now . . .*
> *That little gang of mine . . .*

A roar of applause came up as the spotlight hit me. I could
feel the soft peach chiffon playing around my legs and see the
zircons glittering on my shoulder straps. It was Las Vegas, a
town that loved zircons because zircons had more class than
rhinestones but lacked the permanence of diamonds.

> *. . . Eating fancy chow*
> *and drinking fancy wine.*

Gradually I began to recognize familiar faces at the long
rows of tables topped with fancy chow and fancy wine, and as I
kicked a leg high there was another roll of applause. The inside
of my mouth was like cotton and my stomach lurched. Then quite
suddenly, I was soaring, carried by the music, the words, the
lights, and the velvet darkness of the vast room packed with that
audience that Oscar Hammerstein had once called "the big black
giant." I spread my arms wide and felt joyous and exalted and free.

> *I'd like those stumblebums to see for a fact*
> *The kind of top-drawer, first-rate chums I attract*

Right in front of me were Carroll O'Connor and his wife, Nancy, and behind them, glowing like a golden presence, was Goldie Hawn. Off to my left was Gwen Verdon, red-haired and beautiful, dazzling me with her electric smile, and over to the right was Matty Troy, the Democratic boss of New York's Queens County. I could see Pat Cadell and Fred Dutton, with whom I had traveled through so many strange towns during the tragic McGovern campaign. In another part of the darkened theater were Sam Brown and Dave Mixner, the insistent young men with whom I had marched on Washington to protest the killing in Asia. Lucille Ball sat in a back booth, she who had given me so much laughter and so much instruction; and beside her was Ginger Rogers, who had inspired me to want to dance when I was a little girl. There were dozens and dozens of others, friends from politics and publishing, from newspapers and magazines, from show business, from foreign countries. Top-drawer, first-rate friends. It was as if all the important phases of my life over the past ten years sat before me.

> *All I can say is wow!*
> *Just look at where I am!*
> *Tonight I landed, pow!*
> *Right in a pot of jam!*

I loved the way I felt; strong and resilient and sinuous, with plenty of breath to spare and easy, sharp movements to dance with. There had been a year of running on the beach, long hours spent in sweaty gymnasiums, early mornings in dance studios. I had given up bread, potatoes, Hershey bars with almonds, and homemade chocolate chip cookies—the mainstay of my diet along the campaign trail. No more cigarettes, no more sedentary hours writing a book. The dryness in my mouth vanished and I could feel adrenalin flooding my body. Back in the dressing room there were masses of flowers and hundreds of telegrams from well-wishers. While getting ready I thought about all the people I had met over the past few years and wondered what they were doing this evening: the people I had worked with on my disastrous TV series, all the people of America I had talked with during the campaign, the people I had greeted in strange dusty towns in China. Absurdly, given the setting, I thought of Chou En-lai, who had suffered a heart attack, and pictured his wife, Teng Ying-ch'ao, sitting through the nights with him. I wondered whether either of them could ever understand that my being here, on this huge stage in super-capitalistic Las Vegas, had everything to do with them, and all their comrades.

> *What a set-up! Holy cow.*
> *They'd never believe it . . .*

The dancers were on the stage now. Together we kicked our legs high in the air, kicking for laughter and joy, kicking because we loved to make people feel good, kicking because we loved to feel good ourselves. The audience began to applaud again and we kicked higher. I moved to stage left and suddenly saw Margaret Whitman, silver-haired and dignified, who had been with me in China. I remembered what she had said to a friend that afternoon. "China makes you feel anything is possible. That's why Shirley's here." I had thought about that all day, turning it over in my mind.

With my straw hat raised in the air, I finished the opening number. The final applause was explosive, led by Dan Melnick, the head of MGM, which was no longer a major studio but which ran the hotel in which I was appearing, and I remembered an afternoon a few years before when everything had seemed bleak and forlorn. It was a time when I, like almost everyone I knew, had stopped laughing. Now Dan, sitting next to Kirk Kerkorian, who now owned the company that owned Metro, was laughing. So was every other person in the room. And for some reason, I felt as if I had just begun to live my life again. After a long time away I was back doing what I had been trained to do in the first place. Only now I knew a lot more about who I was because the road back hadn't been an easy one.

As always, Shirley MacLaine brings her special quality of mind and heart to tell this sensitive and profound tale of rediscovery. It is no wonder it was hailed by The New York Times *as "a fascinating book . . . she is an articulate sophisticated woman."*

OUT ON A LIMB

The sophisticate of the seventies became a fascination in the eighties with her 1983 book, which detailed an intimate and powerful journey into her personal life and inner self.

An intense, clandestine love affair with a prominent politician sparks Shirley MacLaine's quest of self-discovery. From Stock-

holm to Hawaii to the mountain vastness of Peru, from disbelief to radiant affirmation, she at last discovers the roots of her very existence.

THAT NIGHT I found myself looking up reincarnation in the encyclopedia.

Let me say that I was not brought up to be a religious person. My parents sent me to church and Sunday school, but it was because it was the accepted place to be on Sundays. I wore crinoline petticoats and tried not to glance too often at the lyrics in the hymnal I was supposed to have memorized. I wondered where the money went after the collection plate was passed, but I really never had any feeling one way or the other whether there was a God or not.

Jesus Christ seemed like a smart, wise, and certainly a good man, but I viewed what I learned about him in the Bible as philosophical, mythological, and somehow detached. What he preached and did didn't really touch *me,* so I didn't believe or disbelieve. He just happened . . . like all of us . . . and he did some good things a long time ago. I took his being the Son of God with a grain of salt and, in fact, by the time I was in my late teens, had decided for myself that God and religion were definitely mythological and if people needed to believe in it that was okay with me, but I couldn't.

I couldn't believe in anything that had no proof and besides, I wasn't all that agonized by the need for a purpose in life or something to believe in besides myself. In short, where religion, faith in God, or the immortality of the soul were concerned, I didn't think much about them. No one insisted and I found the subject boring—not nearly so stimulating as something real and humorous like people. Every now and then as I grew older I would engage in a bemused argument over the pitfalls of such mythological beliefs and how they detracted from the real plight of the human race. I didn't much like the authoritarianism of the church—any church—and I considered it dangerous because it made people afraid they would burn in hell if they didn't believe in heaven.

But as much as I was disinterested in God and religion and the hereafter, there was something I was extremely interested in. From the time I was very young I *was* interested in identity. My identity and that of everyone I met. Identity seemed real to me. Who was I? Who was anyone? Why did I do the things I did? Why did they? Why did I care about some people and not others? The analysis of relationships became a favorite subject of mine—the relationship I had with myself as well as with others.

So maybe because I was interested in the origin of my own identity it intrigued me that there might be more to me than what I was aware of in my conscious mind. Perhaps there were other identities buried deep in my subconscious that I only needed to search for and find. Indeed many times in my work with self-expression, whether dancing, writing, or acting, I would be amazed at myself; baffled as to where a feeling or a memory or an inspiration had come from. I had put it down to a hazy concept called the creative process, as did most of my fellow artists, but I have to admit that at the bottom of whoever I was I felt a flame that I was not able to understand, to touch. What was the origin of that flame? Where did it come from? And what had come before it?

I was always more interested in what went *before* than what might come after. So for that reason, I suppose I wasn't so interested in what would happen to me after I died as I was in what made me the way I was. Therefore when the notion of *life before birth* first struck me I guess you might say I was curious to explore it.

The encyclopedia said that the doctrine of reincarnation went back as far as recorded history. It consisted of belief in the connection of all living things and the gradual purification of the soul, or spirit, of man until it returned to the common source and origin of all life which was God. It was the belief that the soul was immortal and embodied itself time and time again until it morally worked out the purification of itself. It said that the companion subjects of karma—that is, working out one's inner burdens—and reincarnation—the physical opportunity to live through one's karma—were two of the oldest beliefs in the history of mankind and more widely accepted than almost any religious concepts on earth. This was news to me—I had always vaguely connected reincarnation with disembodied spirits, hence ghosts, the occult, and things that go bump in the night. I had never connected it with any major, serious religion.

Then I looked up religion. Although it was impossible to give a conclusive definition, several characteristics were common to most religions. One was belief in the existence of the soul, another the acceptance of supernatural revelation, and finally, among others, the repeated quest for salvation of the soul. From the Egyptians to the Greeks, to the Buddhists and Hindus, the soul was considered a preexistent entity which took up residence in a succession of bodies, becoming incarnate for a period, then spending time in the astral form as a disembodied entity, but reincarnating time and time again. Each religion had its own belief for the origin of the soul, but no religion was without the belief that the soul existed as a part of man and was immortal. And somewhere between Judaism and Christianity, the West had lost the ancient concept of reincarnation.

I closed the encyclopedias and thought for a while.

Hundreds of millions of people believed in the theory of reincarnation (or whatever the term might be) but I, coming from a Christian background, hadn't even known what it actually meant.

I prepared to leave to meet Gerry wondering what else might be going on in this world that I had never thought about before.

By opening her heart, Shirley MacLaine's courage and candor also opens new doors, new insights, new revelations—and a luminous new world she invites us all to share.

DANCING IN THE LIGHT

Her world continued to grow inward as, in 1984, Shirley MacLaine turned fifty years of age, starred on Broadway and won an Oscar. But more importantly, this special time was the year she resumed the spiritual journey that she calls "a celebration of all my 'selves'."

FROM THE VERY BEGINNING, Vassy and I both believed we had known each other in at least one previous lifetime. For that reason as well as many others, we were spiritually compatible. The concepts that I was exploring were not foreign to him. In fact, they were quite traditional among many Russians.

Yet our relationship was colorfully embattled because our personalities were diametrically opposed. Dad was right. Vassy's middle name was suffering and creative conflict, while mine was optimism and positive thinking. The combustion of the two of us together made it impossible to believe that our intense relationship was entirely new. We each knew we were involved in a karmic experience. We believed the intensity existed because we were drawn to work out unresolved aspects, not only with each other but also in ourselves, which the other inspired.

We often spoke of literature being abundant in expressing relationships of love, hate, familial conflict, and fundamentally profound feelings of loneliness, jealousy, power, greed, helplessness, and so on. We felt that great literature was epic because it was really about karma. We believed the experience of life itself was only about working out those conflicts within ourselves, using other human souls as the catalyst.

So, for example, we believed each love affair we experience has its purpose—its reasons for occurring. And on a soul level, we *know* that. The chemistry that draws us to someone is really the memory of having experienced them before, and understanding that there are unresolved areas that need to be concluded.

Our love affair validated that truth very clearly in our view. But as we found ourselves caught up in the throes of the joyful conflict of loving male-female embattlement, we often forgot the fundamental mystique of our attraction in the first place. On the other hand, perhaps living completely in the *now* was the only way we could work out our problems together. In the end, the problems were not about each other. They were about *ourselves,* as I believe all conflicts are.

What fascinated each of us more than anything was the undeniable truth that our relationship was analogous to the conflicts that Russians and Americans were experiencing with each other on a global level. Our relationship was a microcosm of those misunderstandings and cultural differences. But more than that, each of us experienced the conflicts of the male and female energy existent in *each* of us.

Let me begin with our initial meeting.

I was frantically winding up making a movie when actor Jon Voight called and insisted that I see a work by a Russian filmmaker, a friend of his whom I will call Vassily Okhlopkhov-Medvedjatnikov (his real name was just as complicated). Jon said the film was long but brilliant.

I pleaded exhaustion and said I wasn't interested in a ponderous Russian film.

Jon said, "I know, but you'll see something deeply moving. Come. I want you to meet Vassy. Please, do it for me."

On that basis, I went.

Driving along the freeway toward the San Fernando Valley, I should have realized what was about to happen as I relaxed my mind after the insanity of the movie set. I tried to picture what this Russian filmmaker could possibly be like. I had known many Russians when I was in the ballet; I was familiar with and amused by the colorful explosiveness that underlined their lives, and attracted to the passion and deeply felt sensitivity they expressed in their creative arts.

A picture of the Russian director swam into my mind as I drove. I was bemused by the clear definition of the image. Outrageous, I thought to myself.

The figure I imagined was very clear. He was a tall, lean, rather tawny-skinned man with high Mongolian cheekbones and deep brown, fawnlike, almost almond-shaped eyes. He was smiling with a broad, full-toothed grin revealing white teeth, an impressive array engineered to present "perfect imperfection." Why such a sophisticated dental allusion occurred to me, I couldn't imagine. This imposing-looking imaginary male wore a brown leather jacket over loose-fitting blue jeans which were not snug because his hips were slim. In my head I saw him standing in front of my car as I was directed to projection room 1. Brown hair crept over the collar of the leather jacket and every so often he swept hair back from his forehead with a circular movement.

All of this flashed in my mind as I negotiated the evening traffic on the freeway.

I pulled up to the gate at Universal and asked where the screening of the Russian film was because I couldn't remember the man's name. The cop at the gate said projection room 1! A coincidence, I thought to myself.

I rounded the alley looking for it when there in the street in front of my car was a tall, lean man in a brown leather jacket and loose-fitting blue jeans. He was obviously standing in wait for someone. He looked exactly like the man I had "imagined." I could see the high-cheekboned structure of his head, although aviator dark glasses concealed his eyes. Impatiently, with a curved motion, he swept his fingers through his hair. I wondered what the hell was going on while emerging nonchalantly from the car.

He rushed to help me out of it, whipping off his glasses as though he wanted a clearer look at me. I thanked him and looked directly into his eyes. I had the definite feeling that I knew him.

"But the story is not finished," says Shirley MacLaine, "for I am still a woman in search of myself, the lives I might have lived and the inner heart of being." The road to self-discovery was not over.

IT'S ALL IN THE PLAYING

"It began in Peru ten years ago and ended in Peru ten years later. But the steps along the way were the real story."

Here is the fifth volume in Shirley MacLaine's extraordinary adventure, a candid, controversial, and compelling account of her greatest role—as seeker of personal and metaphysical truth. Join her in the journey within . . . and the journey beyond . . .

AFTER WORK THAT NIGHT I went into Hollywood to see *A Chorus Line—The Movie*. It was a balmy soft night when I wandered out of the theater thinking about the film. It brought up so many memories for me, having started in the chorus myself. I stopped on a side street and stood looking into the star-studded sky trying to "remember" whether I had written the scenario of my life before I was born: the struggling, disciplined, dancing days, the night I went on for Carol Haney, the relationship with Alfred Hitchcock, the smiling-through-tears on the silver screen, the adjustment to myself as a communicator, and finally the ventures into travel, politics, writing, and spiritual questing. Did my interest in performing have its genesis in understanding that my life always had been a role I had written long ago to be played out on an earth plane stage today? And had John Heard made his entrance just in time to live up to the part I had written for him in *my* script? And if it was *my* script, then was his character really an aspect of me?

The convolutions of intersecting realities drifted through my mind as I left the side street and walked farther into the balmy "Hollywood" night. Hollywood . . . the most famous center of illusion in the world. And the illusions created on film and stage were alternative realities to me—not really make-believe. When entertainment was good and absorbing, nothing else existed. I forgot my "real" life and focused on another adventure. Was that the same principle by which we experienced lifetimes? A matter of focus?

As I walked I began to speculate on whether my idea of linear reincarnation was a truth or merely a simplification. Using my present lifetime as an analogy to multiple life experiences, I began to wonder about the role that *time* played in my reality.

Einstein had said there was no such thing as time—as we measure it. The spiritual masters confirmed such a concept. They said instead that past, present, and future were the same.

In other words, all time was happening now, and always. Perhaps linear concepts were man's way of dealing with the dumbfounding awesomeness of totality. Our way of measuring time, then, became a way of focusing on aspects of the totality.

If time was happening to us all at once, then perhaps we weren't living linear incarnations one after the other; perhaps we were only *focusing* on one at a time.

As I walked I thought of my own body. It existed in its own totality. I was not aware of specific aspects of my body unless I focused on something I chose. I stopped walking. I focused on my big toe—the big toe of my right foot. I was unaware that my big toe on my right foot was important until I concentrated my attention on it. Then the big toe became paramount in my awareness: a kind of life in itself. Especially if someone should step on it, I thought. I stood still under the stars, focusing on the big toe of my right foot. I was creating that focus.

Perhaps that was what we were doing with each lifetime, each experience being only that which we chose to focus upon. Would that explain our feelings that dreams were real, that visions were real, that fantasies were real? Maybe I was only dipping and overlapping into parallel realities and I was correct in my assumption that *all* of them were real.

When I had premonitions of the future, perhaps I was tapping into an alternative reality which I could only define in a linear manner as the "future," but in actuality it existed simultaneously with the present. When we had *déjà vu* experiences, perhaps we were not actually seeing something in a past/future life sense, but inadvertently shifting to a different aspect of the whole—much as I had (deliberately) focused on my big toe just a moment ago.

So maybe life was essentially a matter of focus in time—analogous to film because films were also an attempt to focus on special moments of a life experience.

Those of us who made films were creating the scenario we wanted to be played out. We knew the best films were karmically balanced (the bad guys always paid). The subjects that attracted audiences were subjects they could identify with and relate to in their own lives. We knew they would suffer with the heroes and heroines because they would see themselves as heroes and heroines of their own drama. And the supporting players would be easy to identify in their own lives as well.

And even though we filmmakers knew that they would know the ending of a movie was intact at the end of the roll of film, we presented it as though it would be a spontaneous experience for them. We expected them to glue themselves to our illusion, allowing the truth of it to function as a separate reality from what they knew was only a movie-making trick. We attempted to create a trick-truth for the audience and we evaluated ourselves by how completely they bought it.

I began to walk again slowly under the stars and palm trees, releasing the focus on my big toe.

So we filmmakers were the purveyors of illusion, using all the tricks of the trade to convince the audience that what they saw was real. And wasn't that what we did with our lives too? We focused on a feeling or an event that created feeling, and we called it reality. We put ourselves through sorrow, exhilaration, anger, love, or whatever, and all of it was only an exercise in searching out who we were more deeply. Was life simply to experience feeling? Was that also the great contribution of films in the world? Did they reflect human emotions back to ourselves, which was just what playing our parts in life accomplished? A certain kind of film had even developed a genre term: "slice of life," meaning no beginning, no middle, no end. Not neat but, like life, just a piece of the whole. We could wander into the middle of any film in much the same way that we could wander into a daydream or a seemingly out-of-context dream at night. We woke in the morning knowing that the dream had occurred, but because of our limited concept of reality we said: "It was only a dream."

I wondered how it would feel, when I finally passed on, if I were to turn around, look at my life, and say "It was only a dream, but it seemed so real."

Copyright © 1987 by Shirley MacLaine

GOING WITHIN

In somewhat of a departure from her other books, Shirley MacLaine's rich and rewarding guide takes readers on their own journey inward. From finding inner peace and awareness to giving us the power to shape our lives, readers learn of transformation and the discovery of a whole new way to live.

I HAVE BEEN HAVING an extraordinary adventure for the past seven years. Some would call it an adventure in cosmic consciousness, and while I would agree with that, I would also add that it is an adventure which enjoys the advantage of extremely pragmatic, down-to-earth application in real life.

I am learning that it is my choice to perceive the world in a more optimistic and positive light because I am learning that it is also my choice to perceive myself that way. Every single day is a lesson in the old adage that the transformation of the world we see begins with the transformation of how we see ourselves. Everything begins at home and the choices we make within the Self.

I used to hear these words and privately feel that this was simple "selfishness" or even dangerously self-centered fantasy. No longer. To me, this concept has become a giant truth. "Know thyself"—and everything else follows. In fact I now realize that it is impossible for me to understand anything of the world, its inhabitants, their suffering, their conflicts or the full potential of life itself until I am in touch with these same currents and truths inside myself. To understand and love others begins with understanding and loving oneself.

These are issues of the spirit, not of the mind and body. When I began the investigation of understanding the spiritual aspect of my nature *and* that of everyone else, the missing pieces of the puzzle of the human condition began to fall into place.

The study took work, discipline, and a concentrated effort in unraveling the ancient techniques of what I call spiritual technology. The more I applied the tools of what I investigated, the more I found my own experience, my own attitudes, and my own perceptions transforming my life into a more positive and peaceful adventure.

As the millennium approaches and a new century beckons, the complications of living are becoming more challenging. Millions of people all over the world are seeking to transform and improve their lives. They are painfully aware that the answers for a changed world are not coming from sources outside of themselves. The answers lie within.

That is what this book is about. GOING WITHIN offers keys for enlightening one's inner perceptions. It is a kind of personal road map for achieving spiritual clarity that can make the transformation in inner attitude improve outer reality. Hopefully my own search, with its methods, techniques, and new approaches can be helpful to those who are also seeking to reduce conflict, anger, confusion and stress in their lives.

This book grew out of the year I spent criss-crossing the country conducting seminars on inner transformation. Never before had I spent such quality time with so many people engaged in their own desire for improvement. The intense, face-to-face contact and sharing of deep, powerful and honest emotional struggles in our dangerously complicated world helped me articulate and shape the journey I was making myself. Together we became more skilled in the techniques of meditation and visualization. Together we deepened our understanding of our intuitive gifts and of the body's esoteric centers of energy and their role in both physical and emotional healing. Together we strengthened our belief that each one of us has the responsibility to create the world in which we choose to live.

I don't expect that any of us will succeed in transforming ourselves into a state of peaceful bliss in this lifetime. But each one of us *can* help to leave a better world fit for our children to live in, a world that is more trusting in the belief that inside each of us is a wealth of power to learn how to love and to change.

This is indeed a difficult and sometimes threatening time for all of us. But it is also an astonishing opportunity for growth if we choose to look at it that way. They very urgency of the need for change will accelerate the metamorphosis required to proceed into the next century and the next millennium.

The longest journey begins with the first step. Perhaps the longest journey is the journey within. It is never too late to begin.

"With all I have done in my life, I have come to the conclusion that the most important journey I have taken is the one into myself," says Shirley MacLaine. "Or, as Yeats said, 'It is not the most important journey, it is the only journey.' "

Discover the startling world of Shirley MacLaine and uncover the world within yourself.

Available wherever Bantam paperbacks are sold.

OUT ON A LIMB

BY SHIRLEY MACLAINE

A voyage into the realm of the mind and the spirit.

In this remarkable and moving story we are invited to accompany world famous actress Shirley MacLaine on a unique journey – to Stockholm, where she meets a trance channeler whose unusual gift opens the door to her past; to Europe and Hawaii, where a secret (and perhaps fated) affair of the heart unfolds; and finally to Peru, where high in the mountains she has a startling out-of-body experience that clarifies for her the extent of human potential and the understanding that the soul lives forever.

Out On A Limb is the deeply personal story of a woman determined to know herself and to become all she is capable of being. Shirley MacLaine, author of two previous best-sellers, *"Don't Fall Off The Mountain"* and *You Can Get There From Here*, has opened her heart more than ever before, and her story is unforgettable.

"Highly Entertaining"
The Guardian

0 553 17201 8

DANCING IN THE LIGHT

BY SHIRLEY MACLAINE

Dancing in the Light begins with Shirley MacLaine's fiftieth birthday celebration. We meet her closest friends and colleagues, experience her relationship with her daughter Sachi, and enter the dazzling world of show business from behind the footlights, guided by one of America's brightest stars.

But this beginning becomes Shirley MacLaine's doorway to the past. Searching for a new understanding with her parents, she talks openly of their loving but stormy relationship, of her childhood and her irresistible drive to perform, and what that means to her, emotionally, physically, and artistically. She actively looks for answers: did she know her parents in a past life? Why is she so drawn to the Russian spirit . . . and did she envision before she ever met him, the handsome young Russian film-maker who became her lover in one of the most volatile, passionate, and intense experiences in her life?

With the help of her spiritual guides, Shirley dares to explore her choices, her beliefs and her conflicts – an exploration that finally leads to sun-drenched Santa Fe for the life-altering experience that provides a remarkable new vision of herself, her future – and the fate of our world.

'A compelling insight into the thoughts and feelings of an unusual, intelligent, sensitive woman whose life is devoted to pushing back the frontiers of all manner of experiences'
Psychic News

0 553 17239 5

IT'S ALL IN THE PLAYING

BY SHIRLEY MACLAINE

The fifth volume in one of the most extraordinary personal odysseys of the twentieth century.

"Don't Fall Off the Mountain", *You Can Get There From Here*, *Out On a Limb*, *Dancing In the Light* and now the most intimate and compelling book of all, *It's All In the Playing*. Oscar-winning actress, social activist, singular entertainer, bestselling author – Shirley MacLaine has the courage to be both candid and controversial. In this book, she casts herself in her most challenging role yet – as seeker of personal and metaphysical truth.

'*It began in Peru ten years ago and ended in Peru ten years later. But the steps along the way were the real story.*' In filming the miniseries *Out On a Limb*, Shirley MacLaine was forced to recreate herself ten years earlier. To journey back from Malibu to London, from Sweden to the mysterious landscape of Peru . . . to the places, the perceptions and profound emotions she experienced then. And to journey beyond, exploring new personal and cosmic dimensions, the choices of her lifetimes, who she was and who she would become. At the heart of Shirley MacLaine's testament is a compelling challenge; We choose our own destinies, create our own illusions. We have the power to design the world in which we live, and the strength to remake ourselves in the image of our dreams.

'Delightful, easy to read, gossipy' – *The Guardian*

0 553 17512 2

A SELECTION OF TITLES AVAILABLE FROM CORGI AND BANTAM BOOKS

THE PRICES SHOWN BELOW WERE CORRECT AT THE TIME OF GOING TO PRESS. HOWEVER TRANSWORLD PUBLISHERS RESERVE THE RIGHT TO SHOW NEW RETAIL PRICES ON COVERS WHICH MAY DIFFER FROM THOSE PREVIOUSLY ADVERTISED IN THE TEXT OR ELSEWHERE.

All Corgi/Bantam Books are available at your bookshop or newsagent, or can be ordered from the following address:
Corgi/Bantam Books,
Cash Sales Department,
P.O. Box 11, Falmouth, Cornwall TR10 9EN

Please send a cheque or postal order (no currency) and allow 80p for postage and packing for the first book plus 20p for each additional book ordered up to a maximum charge of £2.00 in UK.

B.F.P.O. customers please allow 80p for the first book and 20p for each additional book.

Overseas customers, including Eire, please allow £1.50 for postage and packing for the first book, £1.00 for the second book, and 30p for each subsequent title ordered.

NAMF (Block Letters) ....

ADDRESS ....

....